PROFITABLE
PARTNERSHIPS

**Improve Your Franchise Relationships
and Change Your Life**

by

Greg Nathan

Eighth Edition

INSTITUTE

FRANCHISE RELATIONSHIPS INSTITUTE
MELBOURNE AUSTRALIA

This book can be purchased in bulk for distribution to franchise groups. For details contact the publishers:

Franchise Relationships Institute

PO Box 8487
Armadale 3143 Victoria
Australia

Email: info@franchiserelationships.com
Phone: +61 7 3510 9000
Web site: www.franchiserelationships.com

ISBN 0 646 40271 4

Cover: Sue McIver, The Design Group, Queensland, Australia
Layout: Paul Howson, The Design Group, Queensland, Australia
Printed by A&A Printing, Tampa, Florida, USA

National Library of Australia Cataloguing-in-Publication entry

Nathan, Greg, 1955-

Profitable Partnerships: Improve your franchise relationships and change your life.

ISBN 0 646 40271 4.

1. Franchises (Retail trade). 2. Business communication.

I. Title.

658.8708

A Word from the Author

Thank you for reading this eighth edition of *Profitable Partnerships*. I hope you find it useful. We receive a lot of positive feedback from franchisors and franchisees all over the world who say the book has helped them to clarify and put into practice important ideas on how to work together more effectively. This is of course satisfying for an author who has always tried to make a positive difference to the lives of people working in the franchising sector.

I am a psychologist who started in business as a franchisee and later worked in senior franchisor executive roles before consulting with hundreds of franchise companies. Because of my background I tend to draw a lot from first hand personal experience as well as research. For this reason it may be useful to provide a snapshot of my background.

I have always loved music and spent most of my youth playing guitar in garage bands. I also have a long-standing fascination with what makes people tick. So when, as a young adult, I was given the opportunity to pick a University course to study, I chose two — music and psychology. This was probably too ambitious because I struggled to keep up with my studies and earn enough money to support myself. So I dropped the music course and secured a well paying early morning job making bread in a small retail bakery — an interesting balance to my psychology classes.

Little did I know that this fledgling bakery chain had big plans that would one day enable me to play a role in developing the operating systems of what would become a highly successful publicly listed company, Brumby's Bakery. During this time I also met my best friend and wife, Ann, who would sit with me in the cafeteria listening patiently to my endless stream of ideas on how psychology could be used to build a better world.

After graduating I swapped my bakery job for a cushy research post in the Psychology Department at Monash University. But for me the work lacked creative challenge. One of the franchisees I had worked for, John Salomon, heard about my boredom. John offered me a partnership in his business and soon I was a franchisee running three highly profitable stores. I spent the next seven years with Brumby's in various store based and head office roles, including National Marketing and Operations Manager.

Throughout this period I was often puzzled by the nature of the franchise relationship. As a franchisee I was frequently frustrated by my franchisor's inability to explain why we were required to do things a certain way and the benefits I received for my royalty fees. Later as a member of the franchisor team my confusion continued. Is this just a legal agreement or is it more? Are these people our customers? Do they have to do what we tell them? If we are on the same side why are we always arguing? Despite my questions it was hard to find answers that made sense. It seemed that my colleagues in other franchising companies were also struggling with these people issues.

It was the lack of answers that led me to set up a business to find solutions to these challenges. I spent the next ten years running training programs for franchise companies, and researching and writing about the franchise relationship in business magazines. I then set a goal to write a book on the franchise relationship that would be useful to franchisors and franchisees. I wanted to cover all the issues that impact on the franchise relationship from both perspectives while ensuring the book was easy to read. It took around a year to synthesise and simplify my thoughts while maintaining the key concepts.

The first print run of *Profitable Partnerships* sold within weeks and the positive feedback from franchisors and franchisees was overwhelming. This inspired me to establish the Franchise Relationships Institute (FRI), a research and education group with a mission to develop evidence based tools for helping franchisors and franchisees succeed together.

FRI's research has since shown, for people who choose to be part of the franchising sector, the nature of their relationships will have a significant bearing on their success as well as their work and life satisfaction. More importantly, we have also found this to be an area that is both poorly understood and poorly managed. This is what makes our work interesting and motivating.

There are a few people in particular who have helped to turn this vision into a reality. My parents, Shirley and Victor, always encouraged my brother, Rafi, and me to back our own judgment, a quality for which I am extremely grateful. Bob Peterson, Chair of the Franchise Council of Australia (FCA) in the early 1990s, recognised the significance of what I was trying to achieve in my educational work and was very supportive. Stephen Giles and John O'Brien, both Chairs of the FCA, have also supported the ongoing development of our work in Australia and beyond. I am also grateful to Katrina Mitchell, Rupert Barkoff and Stan Freidman for encouraging me to expand FRI's educational work into the USA.

Thanks also to the people within the various franchise sector organisations around the world, too many to mention individually, who have promoted our work to their members and clients, including the Franchise Council of Australia, the International Franchising Association and its ICFE program, the Franchise Association of New Zealand, the American Bar Association's Forum on Franchising, Franchize Partners in South Africa, the Bittencourt Consulting Group in Brazil and Effectum Consulting in Norway.

Finally I would like to thank Paul Howson and Sue Hamlet for their care in designing this book, and to recognise the amazing team at the Franchise Relationships Institute, especially my business partner, Louise Broekman. They handle the complex and demanding nature of our work with a balance of professionalism, creativity and fun. With their support I am able to tour the globe sharing our research findings and spreading the message that constructive franchise relationships matter. Hopefully after reading this book you will agree!

Greg Nathan

April 2015

Contents

Introduction

As you are reading this book I already know something about you; namely you are interested or involved in franchising. You probably also belong to one of the following groups of people for whom this book has been written.

This book is for you

Members of a franchisor management team

The franchisor company is typically regarded as the senior party in the franchise relationship because it has legal ownership of the trademark and business systems (intellectual property) on which the franchise is built. If you are a member of a franchisor team you have a serious responsibility ahead of you. Many people are relying on your competence and the integrity of your franchise system for their success.

Existing or potential franchisees

If you are in this group you currently hold a franchise agreement with a franchisor or perhaps you are considering purchasing a franchise. You may even be a multi-site franchisee running several businesses within the one franchise system.

I have particularly written this book with you all in mind to encourage a fresh perspective on how you can achieve the success you are seeking. Many franchisees sell themselves short when it comes to the contribution they can make and the value they can gain from their franchise system.

Master franchisees and area developers

As a 'Master' you combine the roles and responsibilities of both franchisee and franchisor. By purchasing the rights to develop, market and sublicense a specific territory, you are accountable to your franchisor for developing your market and following the guidelines of the franchise system. However you are also a mini-franchisor in that you are responsible for servicing the needs of the franchisees in your territory. Many master franchisees find themselves feeling like the proverbial 'meat in the sandwich' in their role as a communications middleman between their franchisees and their franchisor.

Advisers or suppliers to the franchise sector

This category also includes people working for government departments. If you belong to this group the book will certainly give you some valuable insights into what makes the dynamic franchise industry tick and how you might best add value through your services. From my own experience, being an adviser or supplier to a successful franchise system will provide you with many rewarding opportunities to develop yourself and your business.

Business people and students interested in 'best practice'

Franchising is well worth learning more about because it has enabled many small and large businesses to achieve best practice in their industry and dominance in their local markets. Not only do franchisees have significantly lower rates of small business failure than independent business operators, they are typically more profitable and have a better quality of life.

Many franchisor companies also achieve growth rates that simply boggle the minds of their non-franchised competitors. John Naisbitt, author of Megatrends, says franchising is the single most powerful marketing method known to modern business. Ongoing analyses by respected economic forecasting groups, such as IBIS Business Information and IHS Economics, confirm this with predictions that franchising will continue to outperform general economic growth indicators.

Awesome power

If you have ever watched an electrician at work you will notice that he or she has a healthy respect for electricity. They never take anything for granted in their work because they understand electricity's incredible power to create or to kill.

Similarly, as a psychologist I have learned to respect the awesome power of relationships to create or destroy—in business and in life. For instance, the quickest and surest way to wreck a marriage or make a sports team, business partnership or organisation vulnerable to failure is to create an environment of poor communication, conflict and mistrust.

The converse is of course also true. Awesome things can happen when people trust each other, communicate effectively and work well together. Take a team of four 'average' executives who have scarce resources but work well together and are committed to a common goal. I guarantee that they will consistently outperform a group of ten or more intelligent and talented high fliers who have extensive resources but compete and undermine each other. Learning how to communicate and work well with other people is not just common sense; it makes excellent business practice, particularly in today's highly networked economy.

Technically speaking

Let's get the technical definitions out of the way early. Franchising is defined by the International Franchise Association as a method of distributing products or services. The two parties under this business arrangement are:

1. the franchisor, who lends their trademark or business system to
2. the franchisee, who pays a royalty and often an initial fee for the right to conduct a business under the franchisor's name and system.

Technically speaking the contract between these two parties is the franchise but most people also refer to the business that the franchisee buys from the franchisor as the franchise. Where the franchisor provides a total package of business systems and ongoing support the process is sometimes referred to as 'full-format franchising'.

Franchises can take different forms and operate in virtually any type of industry; they can also function at different economic levels. The following are the most common types of franchises:

- Manufacturers with the rights to produce under a trade mark, eg. soft drink bottlers, garment manufacturers.

- Wholesalers with an agency to distribute to retailers, eg. spare part distributors, fuel distributors.

- Distributors for manufacturers, eg. mobile phone and computer shops, automobile dealerships, service stations.

- Retail franchises, eg. fast food outlets, furniture stores.

- Service franchises, eg. home services, consulting businesses.

Different perspectives on a good franchise

Whatever the type of business, the nature of the relationship that emerges from the contract between franchisee and franchisor is a fascinating one. It also tends to be described in varying ways depending on whom you are talking to. For the person wanting professional help in deciding whether a particular franchise is a good one this range of views can be confusing. If you are looking to purchase a franchise with a reputable franchise system and ask the question, "Could you give me your view on this franchise?" you are likely to get a range of responses.

A lawyer will probably focus on the intricacies of the franchise contract and the legal obligations of both parties. (Most franchise agreements are incredibly long and complex.) An accountant would be likely to focus more on the royalty payments and return on investment issues. An academic might lead you into a discussion on distribution channels and organisational power theories, while a marketing person will probably look to the strength of the brand, the competition and where the product lifecycle is at.

The view of a franchise consultant or broker is likely to be more optimistic as they will be receiving a commission if you buy the franchise. They will probably point out that the franchise system has a good track record, will lower your risk, and is a great way of being in business for yourself but not by yourself.

All these perspectives have merit. However none of them are completely satisfying because they are each incomplete. Franchising is a highly interdependent relationship between people. If we just look at contracts, finances and markets and ignore the human dimension of franchising — people's feelings, motivations and behaviour — we ignore the heart of the franchise relationship.

To gain insight into the real nature of a franchise relationship you are best to ask an existing franchisee who will say something like the following.

"This is a pretty good business if you follow the basics of the system and I have certainly achieved a lot. But I have to admit that it's been frustrating at times having to comply with the franchisor's ideas when I don't always agree with them."

This perspective is probably the most practical and is the one from which I will largely be operating in this book.

The relationship in practice

While a franchise agreement is an essential component of the franchise partnership because it defines the legal obligations of both parties, legal agreements will never guarantee mutually productive relationships. Cooperation, commitment and communication are the real building blocks of success in a franchise chain. These largely come, not from legal agreements, but from ethical dealings, strong leadership and the mutual respect of each party for the goals of the other.

In searching for a useful way to describe how the business relationship between a franchisor and a franchisee works in practice, the marriage analogy is probably the most useful, largely because of the long-term nature of the relationship and the interdependence of each party on the other. (More of this in Chapters 4, 5 and 6.)

As in marriage, business relationships can sometimes become strained. Communication can break down and before we know it a host of unnecessary petty problems are born. Where a franchise network has developed a system of good internal communications, pressures on one party — rather than becoming a cause for conflict — can provide an opportunity for people to pull together and grow stronger. This is the true spirit of franchising.

Human issues

Although the idea of working together in a commercial partnership to achieve success sounds simple, we don't need to look very hard to find that theory is one thing — practice another. If working together were so easy, our legal institutions would be downsizing like many other industries, rather than struggling to cope with a backlog of unhappy customers waiting to have their day in court.

This book is largely about managing the human issues which tend to bubble to the surface when people with their homes and life savings on the line feel their security is at risk. It is about managing people through change when they are comfortable where they are and don't want to listen to a different view. It is about working with people in a highly interdependent relationship when there are differing views to reconcile. These are the day to day challenges of franchising or indeed any business partnership.

If you learn to understand and skillfully manage these challenges — to harness the power of relationships — you will be rewarded handsomely. I guarantee it. Your staff will respect you and give you their loyalty; your franchisor or franchisees will support you; and your customers will love you and recommend you to their friends. If you want to build a successful business, the ability to build lasting, positive relationships with others is a great place to start.

Wise decisions

The success of a franchise chain also depends heavily on franchisors and franchisees making wise selection decisions. As in the marriage analogy, a systematic and thoughtful approach to franchisee selection will significantly reduce the likelihood of either partner 'marrying the wrong person'.

When serious problems do arise in a franchise chain they can usually be traced to one of three reasons.

Firstly, the franchise may not be commercially viable. This can be due to a number of factors such as an inappropriate site or the product or service no longer being relevant to the needs of the market. (We cover this in Chapter 13.)

Secondly, the franchisee may be unsuitable for the franchise concept. Again this can be due to a number of factors such as unrealistic expectations by the franchisee or their inability to master the skills and attributes needed for success in this type of business. Chapters 7 and 16 have some useful information on franchisee suitability and competence, and how to spot the warning signs of problems in the franchise relationship.

Thirdly, there may have been a breakdown in trust and communication between the franchisee and franchisor leading to a general deterioration in the relationship. You will find throughout the book tips and insights to prevent such a breakdown from occurring.

No jargon —just common sense

You will be pleased to know that I have avoided anything that could be construed as overly complex, intellectual or faddish. Rather our focus will be on practical ideas based on commercial experience, good research and common sense. I have also avoided technical definitions and simply treated franchising as a business process where people come together to grow their sales and expand the market for their goods or services.

Whatever your interest in franchising or your reason for reading this book, I hope its pages help you to find answers to some of the questions everyone in business asks from time to time:

"What do I have to do to resolve this situation?"

"How can I reduce my stress and find greater satisfaction?"

"Why won't people listen to me?"

"How can I run a better business and achieve my goals?"

"How can I get people working together more effectively?"

Most of the material in the book comes from my personal experience as a franchisee, franchisor, corporate adviser and mediator. I have discovered through my work with hundreds of franchisors and franchisees that:

1. Franchise chains are only as strong as their weakest link; and

2. The common challenge faced by all people who earn their livelihood in the dynamic franchising industry is unquestionably how to work together for mutual success and prosperity.

If you can come to grips with these two principles an exciting world of opportunities awaits you.

CHAPTER ONE

Good Relationships Will Make You Money

Welcome to the world of franchising: a place where people invest their hard earned savings in a business opportunity, hoping they will achieve their personal aspirations and financial goals. And where franchise companies strive for market dominance, continually pushing and seeking opportunities to do things better, faster, smarter.

The good, the bad and the ugly

Franchise networks offer entrepreneurs of all shapes and sizes the opportunity to join together in a spirit of cooperation with one objective in mind — to gain a competitive edge — to build a growing base of customers loyal to their brand instead of a competitor's.

But be warned. While franchise networks are exciting places where the spirit of cooperation and competitiveness coexist in harmony and where creativity, vision and enterprise thrive — they can also have a dark side. At times they can be places where emotions run high and cause erratic and aggressive behaviour; where individual egos, intoxicated by the smell of success, grow strong and distort one's sense of importance. And where the competitive spirit can turn in on itself— causing politics, factions and power games.

When franchising networks work well they are magic. Franchisees achieve their goals, franchisors grow their markets and customers enjoy outstanding service and value. Everyone wins. But if people lose sight of the principles that inevitably made the franchise network a success — mutual commitment, cooperation and communication — the success that has been achieved can quickly unravel.

As you read through this chapter and the next you will discover that, although franchising is about good marketing and business practices, franchisees and franchisors are in fact in the relationship business.

Three human needs

We like to believe business is all about rational, bottom line thinking. In reality our decisions are largely driven by strong emotions and needs that are wired into our brains.

My Masters supervisor at Monash University, Professor Maurice Balson, used to say three needs in particular shape most people's behaviour throughout their lives:

Belonging. We all need a sense of belonging — to feel we are connected to and accepted by people we regard as significant in our lives. This drive to belong is behind the creation of tribes, villages, clubs, communities, societies and entire civilisations.

Respect. We all want to be treated with respect — to feel we are worthwhile people. This is how we develop our confidence and self esteem.

Purpose. We all need a sense of purpose in our lives: meaningful goals to work toward and values that we believe in. (See Chapters 14 and 15 for more on this.)

These needs are fundamental to human happiness and wellbeing. They are so powerful that when they are met we are most likely to work at our happy and creative best. But if they are undermined or blocked, we are likely to feel hurt or to behave at our absolute worst. For instance attention seeking, withdrawing communication, power plays, cynicism and seeking revenge are just some of the ways people respond if they feel these basic emotional needs have been abused or neglected.

Think for a moment how many personal or business conflicts you have witnessed or been involved with which were triggered because someone felt he or she had been treated badly. Perhaps they felt rejected or put down; or that they were being asked to compromise on their most deeply held beliefs or values.

The human face of franchising

As franchise organisations face the intense business pressures of operating in changing and competitive markets, people's needs sometimes get forgotten. The human face of franchising gets buried under contracts, manuals and strategies. These are the rational, logical aspects of running a business.

But the efficient management of business issues is only half the job. Franchisors also need to manage the personal and interpersonal side of their organisations. People's emotions, values, perceptions and expectations need to be considered when planning and addressing organisational issues. This includes how the franchisor management team are coping with the pressures they face.

Get the people issues wrong and you can kiss goodbye to the best marketing or business plan in the world.

It's not personal?

The managing director of a large and reputable franchisor company (let's call him George), came to me for advice about a franchisee who was threatening to sue his company for misrepresentation. The franchisee's business had never reached break even and after two years of trading losses and royalty payments not being made, the franchisor had decided to terminate the franchise agreement. George said his company had done everything they could for the franchisee and he could not understand why this person was threatening to sue them.

I called the franchisee and we had a long discussion about what had gone wrong and how he was coping. Toward the end of the call he said to me, "You know Greg, I really appreciate you calling and talking with me about my experience. The thing that has really upset me and my family about this whole situation is that George has not even called or spoken to us to say he is sorry about us losing the business."

When I recounted these comments back to George he absolutely blew me away with his response. "It's not as if it's personal", he said. George had obviously not understood the most basic of all principles in franchising: that to a franchisee who invests his home, his pride and his sense of purpose into a franchise, it is an extremely personal affair. All this franchisee wanted from George was some empathy and acknowledgment of the suffering he and his family were going through.

As it turned out the legal posturing was primarily a way to bring this sense of hurt to the attention of the company. (It is worth noting that the real reason behind most legal claims against doctors is that the doctor has failed to apologise or maintain a respectful, caring relationship with the patient.)

Gaining a competitive edge

Ultimately, the power of franchising is in gaining a competitive edge through the sharing of knowledge and resources; sharing being the operative word. This is probably the most important point in this book so I will repeat it.

The power of franchising is in gaining a competitive edge through the sharing of knowledge and resources.

The franchisees who share their numbers

Most franchise networks hold regular conferences where information sharing is encouraged. One successful franchise network, Bakers Delight, takes this to a whole new level. On each franchisee's lanyard, underneath their name, is a list of their store performance numbers. This includes their percentage revenue increase or decrease on last year, and their net profit percentage. Such transparency of data creates a culture of collaboration and continuous improvement where people want to help and learn from each other.

In a franchise network, when people stop sharing knowledge and resources you no longer have a network, but a bunch of individuals battling it out alone. This is what happens when relationships break down — and the costs are enormous.

The commercial imperative of working together

If you were to ask someone in business how important good relationships are to them, they would probably say something like, "Good relationships make my business dealings more pleasant and this is important to me." While this is no doubt true, pleasant dealings in themselves are not what business is all about. Maintaining good relationships draws on time, energy and resources, all of which are in short supply.

For instance it takes time to carefully word a letter when you are angry with someone when you would much rather just bang out an email letting them know how you feel. It takes courage to phone someone to apologise for a small indiscretion. It takes patience and effort to organise a meeting to discuss how people feel about a new initiative when all you want to do is get on with the 101 things on your list. All these things take time and energy. So the question has to be asked, is it worth it?

My experience is that good relationships in a franchise system are more than just a nice thing to have — they are absolutely essential for the following three commercial reasons.

- They help to keep the communication channels open.

- They help to maintain high levels of motivation and commitment — vital to continuous improvement.

- They prevent disagreements from leading to costly legal disputes.

Some examples may be useful here.

Communicate or perish

Earlier I said that the power of franchising was in gaining a competitive edge through the sharing of knowledge and resources. This simply cannot take place when people stop communicating. In fact any battle strategist will tell you the quickest way to seriously disable an enemy's capabilities is to damage its communications systems.

Unfortunately in many cases the enemy is within. I have regularly been invited into companies because relationship problems between senior people have been undermining communication and the organisation's competitive position.

The directors who wouldn't talk to each other

In one case communication between two key directors had been declining for several months. I advised they should either talk through their differences or one of them should stand down. Rather than having the courage to face their differences and sort things out they decided to ignore one another, hoping the problem would go away. This meant the left hand of the organisation did not know what the right hand was doing. After a series of strategically incompatible decisions the company lost millions of dollars and went into receivership.

We have all seen examples of the mistakes that happen when people who should be working together, do not communicate effectively. Good communication is not just a nice thing to have. It is a commercial necessity.

The value of commitment

Consider the cost to your franchise system if motivation and commitment were to drop. Motivated and committed people drive sales. They contribute their time and energy to improve the franchise system. They attend meetings, participate on working committees and encourage new franchisees to invest in the system.

The motivation and commitment of franchisor executives is especially important for a network's development. Unfortunately, faced with a constant barrage of criticism from franchisees, executives can sometimes become defensive, irritable and lose their objectivity. As a result their initiative and performance may drop.

If the motivation and commitment of franchisees drops, a host of crises tend to emerge. People stop taking responsibility for business performance. Rather than being problem solvers, they become problem finders. Instead of defending the system, franchisees start to find fault with it. Take the following example.

The franchisees who went on a motivational strike

The franchisees of a large retail food group were facing declining sales due to some clever new marketing by their major competitor. Yet at this critical time the majority of franchisees decided to no longer attend regional meetings with their franchisor. This decision came about because they felt the franchisor management team always talked down to them and never listened to their ideas. Some of the more vocal franchisees told me they found their franchisor's behaviour particularly offensive because they believed the management team were out of touch with what was happening at the coal face.

As a result they started to criticise and nitpick at every new initiative the franchisor introduced. It became their mission in life to punish their franchisor for not treating them with respect.

The franchisor team, sick of the criticism they were receiving and annoyed at the drop in attendance at the regional meetings, took a short sighted, defensive position and decided to disband the meetings.

I asked the General Manager why he had taken this approach. He claimed the drop in sales was the fault of the franchisees and that he was happy to save the $8,000 that each regional meeting typically cost him.

I suggested this would not only further weaken his already fragile relationship with his franchisees, but that it would actually contribute to their downward sales spiral. I asked him to consider whether the answer to his problems might lie with his franchisees. Rather than relying on the company's marketing experts to come up with the answers, why not put the problems on the table for open discussion? After all, the problem belonged to the whole group and everyone would surely be motivated to find a solution.

He agreed to give it a try and we organised an open forum with a lot of franchisee led discussion. Although many good ideas were collected and later refined and used in the group's marketing programs, something more significant happened: the enthusiasm and morale of franchisees took a significant boost.

Almost immediately the sales decline was reversed as franchisees regained their willingness to share ideas, help each other and work with, rather than against, the franchisor team. As they discussed ideas and explained what they wanted from each other, their frustration subsided and they once again remembered that only by working together could they hope to rebuild their competitive position. They all once again embraced the principle that franchising is about the sharing of knowledge and resources to gain a competitive edge in the market.

Good relationships prevent costly disputes

Another reason to maintain good relationships is that they are the simplest and most cost effective way to avoid legal disputes and save money. Relationship breakdowns can cost those involved tens of thousands of dollars in wasted legal fees — wasted, because rarely does anyone within the franchise network win. When communication breaks down everyone is a loser — perhaps with the exception of the legal fraternity.

To add insult to injury, the bitter experience of unfortunate franchisees and franchisors who have become embroiled in litigation shows that the hidden costs of disputes are often far greater than the legal fees. Ask anyone who has been involved in a serious dispute; they will tell you that people in their businesses literally spent hundreds of hours in meetings, collecting files, writing letters and planning tactics for defending their position. What a waste of time and creative energy which could have been spent on developing everyone's business.

The fact is that most businesses simply cannot afford the luxury of disputation. Whenever you are not involved in value adding activities such as servicing customers, strategic planning or motivating staff, you are inevitably wasting time and money.

The market is not interested in whether or not you are having disagreements with your franchisee or franchisor. While you fight, your competitors will be moving forward and your customers will be left wondering what is going on. The emotional baggage resulting from soured business relationships can also hang around for years and seriously undermine people's ability to maintain a positive focus on the future.

The successful barrister who didn't want to litigate

I once shared the platform at a franchising seminar with a leading barrister who had represented some franchisees in a large and protracted legal dispute. He won the case and his clients were awarded hundreds of thousands of dollars. Yet to my surprise he made the following statement.

"You are an idiot if you think litigation is going to solve your problems."

He went on to make the point that in his experience, when a dispute goes to court he is typically the only person to come out commercially on top. He said that it was far more commercially sensible for franchisors and franchisees to sort out their differences through straight talking, perhaps with the use of a mediator where necessary. He also said it was ironic that although his clients 'won' the case, most never received the agreed settlement money and some went bankrupt along with the franchisor. He added wryly that he earned his living from people who were determined not to use their common sense.

In this particular case, three million dollars were spent on legal fees over a four year period. Surely this money could have been put to better use.

Two sides to every dispute

I am not saying that litigation has no place in franchising, especially if fraudulent or criminal tactics have been used. However at this point I want to share with you a favourite saying, introduced to me by one of my mentors, Dr Bob Dick, a leading thinker in the psychology of groups.

When perception meets reality, reality always comes out second best.

In other words the case that people build up in their own minds regarding the bad behaviour of another party is seldom as cut and dried as they may like to believe. There are always two or more sides to every dispute. An obsession with 'being right' is usually a childish and wasteful use of one's time, money and energy.

The First Step Process

Fastway, a successful courier company with over 1,500 franchisees in 5 countries, has developed a simple but effective process for nipping problems in the bud, which they call the First Step Process.

Fastway's Founder, Bill McGowan, explains the system this way.

"It is written in our franchise agreement that any franchisee who has a problem must have a meeting with an independent chairman within 48 hours. The meeting is also held in an independent environment conducive to relaxed discussion — for instance in a coffee shop.

"The chairperson, who must be acceptable to both parties, is usually a retired accountant or an astute, level headed business person who can create a calm atmosphere and a free flowing discussion. It is deliberately unstructured and offers people maximum control in trying to come to a mutually satisfying agreement. We find it is best to keep the first meeting to less than 2 hours, because after this discussions simply go around in circles and try people's patience.

"We strongly recommend that a lawyer is not used as a chairperson and that lawyers not be allowed to participate in this process. Our experience has been that when lawyers become involved the situation tends to escalate.

"At the end of the round table meeting the chairperson prepares a brief report for all parties, including our Franchise Support Office. If the first meeting doesn't get anywhere the chairperson contacts the parties to arrange another meeting within 48 hours. We have found that if the situation drags on more than that, the chances of a resolution become more remote."

Bill McGowan points out that their First Step Process costs just $50 for each party compared with around $1,000 for formal mediation and over $50,000 if a situation were to escalate into formal litigation.

In summary

Although we like to believe that business is just about rational thinking, our decisions are often driven by emotional needs. It is in fact the passion to succeed that motivates most people in a franchise system to work as hard as they do. While sales and profits may be important goals, you will never achieve them without investing consistently in your relationships with others.

Action Tips:

- Keep sight of the values that have made your franchise business or system a success and reward people for putting these into practice.

- Treat people with respect by listening to their point of view and stay open to their ideas, even when these run counter to your own.

- Get to know the goals of your franchisor or franchisees and do whatever you can to help them achieve these.

- Acknowledge the personal hurts of others and, where appropriate, say you are sorry.

- Encourage and participate in working groups for improving marketing, product development and operational systems.

- Support people who are prepared to take responsibility for improving your business or franchise system.

- Maintain open communication channels at all times, no matter how frustrated you feel. Call in a facilitator if necessary.

- Don't invest time or money in trying to solve relationship or communication problems with legal solutions.

CHAPTER TWO

Understanding the Two Businesses of Franchising

In the last chapter we said that the power of franchising is in gaining a competitive edge through the sharing of knowledge and resources. In this chapter we will look at the relationship between franchising and customer service.

What business are you in?

The first question that any good marketer will ask you is, "What business are you really in?". What they are asking is not "What products do you sell?" but "What customer needs do you meet?". If you can answer this important question with confidence and clarity, then you are well on the way to solving every marketing challenge your franchise network faces. Because marketing is about meeting customer needs while making a profit.

Regardless of the products or services you sell — food, printing, jewellery, furniture, home services, brake repairs —you are basically meeting people's needs. After all, we all want to have more leisure time, communicate better, look good, have an attractive home, travel safely and so on.

The lesson here is that you will only remain successful as long as you continue to provide solutions to your customers' problems or needs in a way that keeps them loyal to your brand. And of course, you must also make a profit. In this sense we are all in the customer service business.

Consistent customer service

To succeed in the business of customer service you need a range of skills and attributes specific to your industry. For instance, if you are in the 'safety business' by offering automotive brake repairs you must have high levels of mechanical expertise. If you are in the 'good impressions business' by offering printing services you must have printing expertise.

If good customer service is about providing solutions to your customers' problems or needs, bad customer service is about customers not receiving what they expect, causing disappointment and frustration. While providing bad customer service is a stupid way to do business because it is almost guaranteed to lead to a drop in sales, it has a more insidious and dangerous side. Bad customer service will inevitably lead to a poisoning of your brand. This is why it is so vital that everyone in a franchise network is committed to maintaining consistent standards of service delivery. After all it is the brand that binds everyone together.

People love to talk

People like to exchange information about products and services. They pass this knowledge on to one another at dinner parties and barbecues, at work and at school, over the phone with friends and family, and of course through social media.

In particular, people love to share their bad experiences. One person who has had a bad experience with your brand will inevitably tell many others. While customer service research has indicated that a dissatisfied customer will on average, tell 12 people of their unhappy experience, the digital world has created a new set of rules for communicating our experiences. Unhappy customers can now instantly share their thoughts and feelings with thousands of people.

There has also been a shift in the psychology of customers. There is far more cynicism today towards corporate messages and, rather than just believe your advertising, customers prefer to listen to each other.

Rational arguments put out by your official public relations machine will always lose when pitted against rumours, because rumours and hearsay will be seen as a more credible source of information. Perhaps this has always been the case; however today rumours travel much faster. The cleverest public relations program in the world can be quickly undermined by the power of people communicating with each other through social media.

Lessons from McLibel

The point is that in this age of instant communications a negative message about your brand can swiftly spread, not just around the neighborhood, but around the globe. McDonalds experienced this during the famous 'McLibel Trial' in the UK when they launched a libel case against two people who refused to stop handing out leaflets that levelled serious criticisms against the company.

While these two detractors had no money or corporate resources behind them, they used social media to gain a high level of international awareness and support for their cause. Although McDonalds won the main points in the libel case, it was a public relations nightmare that reportedly cost them dearly in legal fees and management focus.

The customer who ate maggots

One of the most memorable phone calls I ever received was when I was marketing manager with a retail bakery franchise network. A fellow with a deceptively quiet voice wanted to talk with someone 'high up' in customer service. Let's call him Mr Smith.

The conversation started like this. "I am calling you about an extremely unpleasant experience I have had with your products. It has had a significant impact on my life and I am informing you as a courtesy before contacting my attorney".

I thanked him for calling and asked him to please continue.

"Yesterday morning I purchased a meat pie from one of your stores ..." He paused. "After a couple of mouthfuls I realised that it had maggots in it".

Now he really had my attention.

Mr Smith continued to tell me that he had always loved meat pies but that as a result of his experience he did not think he would ever be able to eat another meat pie again!

As he explained his situation my mind flashed back to discussions I had earlier in the year with the franchisee who owned the store in question. He had asked if he could produce his own meat pies on the premises rather than buy them from our recommended wholesaler. I was initially reluctant but was swayed by their arguments of the lower cost of goods and increased profitability.

My mind was also weighing up the implications of the situation. Assuming his story was true, not only did we have a traumatised customer, disgusted at our company and its products — we were also looking down the barrel of a potential lawsuit.

As it turned out, these two issues were not the real problem.

I listened to Mr Smith, empathised with his feelings of shock and anger, and reassured him that a full investigation would immediately be undertaken. We talked again several times that morning and he finally said that he had decided not to press for legal damages for the time being.

What he did not tell me was that his wife had rung the local television station. That night, one of the headlines in the evening regional television news went something like this.

"A customer got more than he bargained for this morning when biting into a pie from his local bakery."

The story ran with film footage of the store, with signage and brand fully visible, and the partly eaten product. Not surprisingly, sales in this store plummeted; particularly pie sales. But the sales of all products in all our surrounding stores also took a dive. It took several months and a significant investment in advertising dollars to reestablish sales and profitability in these stores.

This story is a typical example of the dangers inherent in sharing a brand.

Neglect standards at your peril

Maintaining the integrity of the brand is everyone's responsibility. When a brand receives bad publicity, even if this is due to one person's behaviour, everyone's business in the network is potentially at risk.

Similarly, the maintenance of quality standards and adherence to operating procedures are everyone's responsibility. Franchisees and even field managers can sometimes regard site inspection reports as overly intrusive and a waste of time. Franchisees might complain, "my sales are down and all you can do is ask me whether my toilets were cleaned today — give me a break!" However adherence to customer service standards should be regarded as an essential and strategically significant maintenance activity in every franchise system. Neglect them at your peril.

Franchisors should also think very carefully before doing special deals or compromising on standard operating systems to satisfy the short-term needs of a franchisee. They may be putting their entire system at risk.

The different contribution of each party

It can be seen that irrespective of the industry you are in or the products or services you sell, if you operate as part of a franchise network you are in an interdependent business relationship. **As well as being in the customer service business you are also in the franchising business.** Many franchisors and franchisees fail to appreciate this and therefore down play the significance of the franchise relationship. Both parties also frequently lose sight of the different contribution each makes to the success of the total system.

If you are in the role of franchisor your job is to help your franchisees achieve their reasonable personal and financial goals. For instance franchisees might expect to achieve success, improved quality of life and a reasonable return on their investment, amongst other things. They rely on you to provide them with the systems, support and advice that will help them to run a successful business and meet these needs.

On the other hand, if you are in the role of franchisee your job is to support your franchisor's systems and maximise sales in your local market. Franchisors will be driving for market growth and positive brand awareness. They are relying on you to deliver on the values of the brand — for example speed, cleanliness, friendliness or reliability — and to cooperate in maintaining the systems and standards they have carefully developed through years of research and experience.

In other words, for the franchise relationship to work effectively, each party expects cooperation and support from the other in meeting its needs.

When one or both parties become unclear of their obligations, problems emerge. These can include frustration over un-met expectations, poor strategy development, inconsistent customer service delivery and confusion over the allocation of resources. Maintaining clarity over the roles of franchisee and franchisor is thus very important.

The franchisee's role

A franchisee has three distinct areas of responsibility. These are to:
• Run a profitable business.
• Grow a base of happy customers.
• Support the franchisor's brand.

Because of their importance, these three areas deserve explanation.

Running a profitable business

If you are a franchisee you are responsible for maximising the local business opportunities in your area, controlling your expenses and managing your business effectively. The franchisor cannot do this for you.

If you are having difficulties achieving your profitability goals there are only three things you can do to change your situation: sell to more customers, increase your prices or reduce your costs. While your franchisor may be able to facilitate some movement in these areas such as generating more customer enquiry through more effective group advertising, or achieving better supply deals, ultimately you have the greatest control over whether sales are achieved or costs are contained. Our research clearly shows that the sales increases achieved by the highest performing franchisees come through their own local marketing efforts. (See also Chapter 16 where we look at the attributes of high performing franchisees.)

Growing a base of happy customers

Because the franchisor does not have direct contact with customers, it has very limited power to impact on a customer's buying experience. It is the franchisee or their staff that interact with the customer. Clearly then the franchisee is responsible for delivering the type of customer service that will keep their customers happy and satisfied so that they will not only return, but will recommend the business to others.

The only way you can grow your business in the long term as a franchisee is to grow a base of happy customers.

Supporting the franchisor's brand

What do you want your customers to think and feel when they see your brand? This is your reputation.

A franchisor's corporate marketing program will usually be based on a promise to the customer. This promise may for instance be related to a higher standard of product quality, faster service or greater reliability than what competitors are offering. If a franchisee does not deliver on this promise they are undermining the brand's reputation. While you may wish your customers to think 'quick and clean' when they see your brand, their actual experience of dealing with a franchisee may leave them thinking 'rough and unreliable'!

The journalist who blew smoke

As mentioned earlier, I have come across numerous cases where the sloppy or careless actions of one franchisee have damaged the credibility of their franchise brand. This of course negatively rubs off on their peers' businesses.

In one case a customer returned to a specialist brake repair outlet because after picking up his car it was blowing blue smoke when he put on the brakes. This outlet was part of a 120 strong franchise network. When he raised his safety concerns with the person at the counter he was told it was not a problem and to go home. After insisting that as far as he was concerned it was a problem, an argument ensued and the customer stormed off in a huff.

As it happened he was a widely read columnist for a major daily newspaper. With great delight this customer/journalist wrote a full page article giving a blow by blow account of his unhappy experience dealing with this particular franchise, brand and all.

It turned out that the franchisee of this store was on holidays and had left his son to manage the business. The son, who was obviously having a bad day, had taken his frustration out on this customer in the form of a full on argument. The son probably thought for a time that he won that one! I don't think however his father or the other 119 franchisees were very impressed.

So while franchisors might have systems in place to ensure a high level of consistently in the delivery of their customer promise, it is the franchisee's job to support and implement this promise.

The franchisor's role

I mentioned earlier that the franchisee has three roles. The franchisor also has three distinct areas of responsibility. These are to:
• Provide credible, positive leadership.

• Help franchisees achieve their financial and personal goals.

• Protect the strategic position of the brand.

Credible and positive leadership

Over the years we have conducted research into what promotes or detracts from franchisee satisfaction. One of the most important factors is credible leadership, which has the following six components.

1. Vision and goals

Defining and sharing the vision for the franchise network. This includes specific long-term and short-term goals to do with market share, numbers of franchises, product development, service delivery and other marketing issues.

2. Competence

Ensuring there is a competent senior management team in place that can handle the strategic and operational demands of the business. Competent managers respond intelligently to franchisee requests for information, are able to discriminate between important and trivial issues, and have the knowledge and skills to ensure projects are completed to a high standard.

3. Integrity

Being honest and trustworthy in one's dealings and delivering on one's promises.

4. Consistency

Being fair and consistent with decisions. Inconsistency, favouritism or 'sweetheart deals' do not go down well in a franchise network and inevitably backfire on all involved. The franchisor also has to be prepared to take a stand on important issues. Sometimes this means an unpopular decision must be made. Franchisees will generally support such decisions if the franchisor is acting fairly and in the best interests of the network.

5. Enthusiasm

Franchisees expect their franchisor to be enthusiastic and positive in its dealings with them. An important role of the franchisor is to motivate and remind franchisees about the benefits of complying with the system. There is no place for dour, negative or lethargic behaviour from anyone on a franchisor management team.

6. Care

Showing a genuine interest in the performance and success of franchisees, particularly their profitability.

Helping franchisees achieve their goals

Good franchisor companies continually ask, "how can we help our franchisees to be more successful?".

Firstly they ensure their franchise systems, marketing programs and field support are all adding value to the franchisees' businesses. They also continually seek opportunities to enhance franchisee profitability through supplier negotiations and continuous improvement initiatives.

Franchisees also like to have the opportunity to contribute their ideas and share the things that have helped *them* to be successful. Participation in committees and discussions at conferences and meetings all help to generate a greater feeling of franchisee involvement and achievement.

Protecting the strategic position of the brand

One of the franchisor's most important responsibilities is to protect the strategic position of the brand. They must firstly define and communicate what the brand stands for. This can be a challenging process that requires in depth thinking and discussion. The franchisor must then keep abreast of changing market trends and ensure it is positioning and promoting its brand in a way that fits the expectations and needs of the target market. They also need to identify the group's sustainable competitive advantage and communicate this clearly to franchisees and customers through relentless internal and external marketing and communication programs.

Brands are like children who need constant monitoring and care if they are to grow and develop in a healthy way. Good parenting involves having a clear vision of the sort of values and behaviours you wish your children to embrace. A child that is neglected or fails to receive adequate guidance or care is at risk of adopting values and behaviours that are inconsistent with its parent's wishes. The same principle is true of brand management. The franchisor is like the parent of the brand. A franchisor that allows their brand to become 'bastardised' is simply not fulfilling one of its most important responsibilities.

In summary

Franchisors and franchisees are in two businesses — the customer service business and the relationship business. Success depends on the franchise system having a relevant customer promise and everyone appreciating their important role in delivering on this. Never forget that one weak link can have disastrous consequences.

Action Tips:

- Be clear on the customer needs that you satisfy and be open to new and innovative ways of meeting these needs.

- Define and consistently communicate your brand values to franchisees and customers.

- Maintain high levels of expertise in the areas that enable you to fulfil your customer promise.

- Never compromise on standards of service delivery or accept this from anyone in your franchise system.

- Do whatever you need to do immediately to resolve the concerns of an unhappy customer.

- Have a clear understanding of your obligations, whether you are a franchisee or franchisor, and take responsibility for fulfilling your unique role in the total franchise system.

CHAPTER THREE

Confessions of the Franchisee from Hell

The previous chapter emphasised the benefits of franchisees and franchisors working together and sharing information. However, be warned. Putting these ideas into practice is not as easy as it sounds. Logic is all very well, however there are forces at work which make this an ongoing challenge for both parties.

As much of the material in this book has been drawn from practical experience, I thought it might be useful to briefly share my story as a franchisee and franchisor with a retail bakery group. My point in doing this is to illustrate some of the important psychological and relationship principles that have great relevance to the franchising environment.

The franchisee from hell

As a franchisee I developed a reputation as a pushy know-it-all. You might have called me the franchisee from hell. My area manager at the time has since recounted how little he enjoyed his visits to my franchise, particularly my complaints of franchisor incompetence and unfair royalty fees. However from my point of view, I was entitled to complain as I was operating the most successful retail bakery in the national group. And my hard work was paying his wages.

My day would start at 2.30am. Our small team would diligently mix, mould and bake a delicious range of breads and pastries. By 9.00am the store would be filled with the aroma and splendour of warm breads and pastries.

Despite the unusual hours and hard work, running a bakery has its rewards. There are not many jobs where everyday, you have the opportunity to create a wide range of attractive products that customers actually enjoy coming into your store to buy. (Most people find buying hot breads and pastries to be a delightful and even sensuous experience.)

Keeping customers happy

As you can imagine, the biggest challenge in a business where all products are made fresh daily is deciding the right amount to produce. To this end I would sit up late at night going through past production sheets, analysing weather patterns and anything else that seemed to influence customer buying habits. Although I was comfortable donating our unsold products to local charities, our waste obviously needed to be kept within specific guidelines.

Yet I understood that, above all, my most important role as a franchisee was to create loyal and happy customers; and to do this I had to ensure we always had enough products on the shelves to satisfy their needs. It was unacceptable to me if a customer left our store disappointed because we had either run out of their favourite products or we could not give them something that would at least get them by.

So it was always with great anticipation that I would arrive back at the store each afternoon to see what we had sold and what was left.

The self-serving bias

If the waste was within our targeted range and the end of day figures were good, I was happy. No thanks to my franchisor of course. It was **my** hard work and entrepreneurial talents that drove the growth and success of my business.

If waste was high or sales were below expectations I tended to brood until I found something or someone to blame. Human nature being what it is, I would scan the environment searching for a suitable target. The franchisor was typically fair game. After all, they were always telling me how great their marketing and sales projection systems were.

Psychologists call this the 'Self-Serving Bias'. It is the tendency that most of us have to take the credit when things go our way, but to blame other people or events when things don't work out as we had hoped. We will revisit this tendency in the next chapter because it goes to the heart of many of the problems that arise in the franchise relationship.

From franchisee to franchisor

As I got smarter at running the businesses, my discontent over the performance and policies of the franchisor grew. I would think to myself, "My staff and I are working our guts out while the franchisor takes 8% of our profit. And for what? It is not as if they are working with me in my store!"

Soon I was voicing my frustration. I also began to resent the franchisor management team who I perceived as lazy, out of touch and making an unreasonable profit on some of our corporate supplies.

In retrospect my franchisor cleverly handled my tendency to 'push the edges of the envelope'. Someone identified my talents for innovation and my store was subsequently used for new product development. I was also asked to assist with the opening of a new concept store.

Although this kept me challenged and busy, I was still looking for more of a challenge. This came in the form of a job offer to join the franchisor team as a State Manager.

Over subsequent months in my new franchisor role I regularly found myself on the other end of heated complaints, most of which I had previously made as a franchisee! However this time I could see that there were good reasons for decisions being made by the franchisor. And far from being lazy, out of touch or uncaring, the franchisor team worked long and hard, and cared passionately for the profitability and welfare of all franchisees.

When I left this company many years later to do consulting work I discovered to my amazement that the people in nearly every franchise company I worked with were having similar experiences. It was as if the play was the same but the actors were different.

The landlord who lost face

On my very first day as State Manager, an incident occured that I will never forget. As I sat at my desk wondering what I should do first, a letter at the top of the correspondence tray caught my eye. It was from a firm of solicitors stating that one of our best performing franchisees in one of our best sites was to lose the lease on his premises.

I called the solicitor whose name was at the bottom of the letter. It emerged that the lease was not going to be renewed because of a minor technicality. Normally this would be overlooked however he explained that his client, the landlord, had a problem with our company, on which he would not elaborate.

So I called the landlord. He initially did not want to discuss the matter, but on hearing my genuine dismay and the fact that I was new in the job he reluctantly agreed to a meeting. At the meeting I discovered a classic case of poor relationship management resulting in significant commercial and emotional disruption. I have since observed this many times in commercial relationships that are interdependent by nature, such as franchising.

It works something like this. Two parties negotiate over an issue. One party in a stronger position at the time pushes too hard or fails to recognise that they have offended or embarrassed the other. It may have been a throwaway comment or a lack of respect in their behaviour. The meeting ends with no genuine resolution to the tension. While the stronger party leaves with an illusion of victory or success, the other is left with a sense of injustice or damaged pride. Because of the interdependence of the relationship the feelings of resentment sit and fester. The 'loser' waits for a suitable opportunity to punish the person or organisation they feel treated them unfairly. It's a case of 'don't get mad, get even'.

This is what had happened in the case of our landlord. He had felt that our organisation had treated him with disrespect in the lease negotiations three years earlier, which had left him annoyed and determined to teach us a lesson. This lesson looked like it was going to cost one of our franchisees his highly profitable business.

In cases where trust or respect has been breached, it is amazing how a genuine apology can put things right. As it emerged the landlord agreed to accept our apology and a new lease was negotiated.

The point is that you should never underestimate the importance of maintaining mature and respectful relationships with your business partners. While this includes suppliers it is particularly true if you are one of the parties in the interdependent franchise relationship.

Domineering people

You have no doubt come across the idea that people have different personalities or behavioural styles. While there are many systems for categorising people into types, I won't go into these here except to say that most systems describe a particular type of person that is relevant to our discussions. These people are easily angered when their efforts are blocked or they don't get their own way. They are enterprising, hard working and like to be in control. They can also be impatient, domineering and demanding in their interactions with others. You have probably worked for someone like this at some stage — or maybe you are like this yourself.

While this type of person will yell and blow off steam when they are frustrated, ten minutes later they are likely to be calm and focussed on something else, as if nothing had happened. If you ask them if everything's okay they might smile and look at you with surprise. The problem is that others who were in the firing line of their tantrum can be left in a quivering mess or feeling angry and resentful.

While people with this habitual behaviour only make up about 15% of the population, most of us do have periods when things just get too much and we feel compelled to let fly. It might be that something really important has been messed up by someone's thoughtlessness or incompetence, or you feel offended by a critical remark.

Why aggressive behaviour is not useful

No matter how aggrieved you feel I have learned that venting your spleen is not a useful thing to do. For instance say you are a franchisee who is angry about something that has happened (or not happened) and you react by aggressively complaining or attacking franchisor staff. Not only will you undermine your relationship with your franchisor, but you also may unwittingly have a negative impact on the whole system.

I have seen several cases where highly talented franchisor staff have resigned after receiving an unfair roasting from an emotional and angry franchisee. In these situations the staff member had little or no control over the events that had led to the franchisee being so angry. In one case the franchisee was acting from totally wrong information and failed to apologise, even when he realised his mistake. The whole franchise network suffers as a result of such cases.

No matter how angry or frustrated you feel about an issue, aggressive behaviour is not useful for the following three reasons.

Firstly, it tends to make the other party less likely to want to deal with you in the future. This means they may not go out of their way to share information that could be useful to you.

Secondly, it makes people less likely to be naturally open and creative if they have to deal with you. You are likely to just get the minimum level of service.

Thirdly, while you might enjoy the short-term satisfaction of having vented your spleen, the person on the other end may take hours or even days to regain their confidence. This can have a significant impact on their productivity and morale.

Of course this message is just as relevant to franchisor executives who feel that venting their frustration at franchisees is going to produce some sort of positive change.

How to let off steam safely

While we will come back to this issue of managing conflict in later chapters, here are a few tips I have found to be helpful if you think you are about to blow your top.

- Call a break to the discussion. If things are getting really tense this can help everyone to save face. You can say something like, "I'd like to think about this and talk to you again tomorrow. Is that okay?" You will find that with a few hours buffer, things don't look nearly as bad.

- Don't assume that the other person knows they have done anything wrong. They may be genuinely ignorant of how their actions have upset you. So take a few minutes to find out why they did what they did. For instance, ask a few questions to better understand the situation from their point of view.

- Consider that you may not be as totally right as you think you are. While you may feel indignant, your perspective is limited to the information to which you have access. There is probably more to this situation than you are aware of so make sure you have all the facts.

- Before launching with all barrels blazing, try to find some more creative ways to get your point across. For instance, wit and humour (but not sarcasm) are less threatening and far more powerful methods of communication.

- Ask yourself this question; "Is damaging my long-term relationship with this person really worth the short-term satisfaction of letting off steam?"

In summary

There is a natural human tendency to take the credit when things go our way but to blame others when things don't work out as we had hoped. People can also be extremely unforgiving if their needs are not met or if they feel they have lost face in a negotiation. Franchisees, with a high emotional commitment to their business, can also become angry and critical if they believe they are not getting the service or support they deserve.

Action Tips:

- Don't take it personally if you are a franchisor and a franchisee is giving you a hard time.

- Acknowledge the contribution of others to your success.

- Harness the energy of creative franchisees by involving them in new initiatives.

- Resolve any unfinished business resulting from a tense negotiation by being generous or gracious in your behaviour.

- Don't be too proud to apologise for any inconvenience or loss you have caused others through your behaviour.

- Maintain mature, respectful relationships with everyone. You never know when you may need their support in the future.

- Accept that it is the nature of some people to blow their stack. You won't get burnt if you just let their steam blow past you.

- If you start to feel angry, avoid showing your aggression. Take a break, check your assumptions and look at the situation from the other person's point of view.

CHAPTER FOUR

Dispelling Some Common Myths

No matter how crazy you think someone is, all human behaviour makes sense when you understand it from the point of view of the person concerned. I regularly receive calls from people who are frustrated, surprised or confused by the behaviour of their franchise partners. In most cases the cause of their problem is faulty beliefs about their relationship that are making them vulnerable to disappointment. In this and the next chapter we are going to dispel some common myths about the franchise relationship.

The myth of independence

Independence is something human beings strive for throughout their lives. Yet the plain fact is that we will always be to a greater or lesser extent dependent on others.

In family situations we depend on our partners and our children, and of course, they also depend on us. People in families depend on each other for emotional support, assistance with household chores and help with finances. Because this dependency cuts both ways we could say people in families have an interdependent relationship.

In business the same principles apply. A pharmacist who runs her own chemist shop may think she is an **inter**dependent business owner. But we all know what happens in business if customers decide not to buy from us any more. The truth is that the so-called independent business owner is highly dependent on his or her customers.

And our suppliers, are they dependent on us? Indeed yes. But we are also dependent on them to provide us with agreed levels of service and consistent quality products. If they let us down we will let down our customers. With suppliers and small business owners the principle of interdependence again emerges. Think about all the businesses and people you rely on for supplies and referrals.

The maturing of independence

There are broadly three types of relationships:
- Dependent (I need you)

- Independent (I don't need you)

- Interdependent (we can achieve a lot more together than we can independently).

In Chapter 8 we will cover the 'E-Factor' and you will see that all three types of relationships have a place in franchising. However the point to note here is that people who think they can be successful in business through an independent, 'I don't need you', relationship are kidding themselves. In all walks of life, personal and business, there are times when we are dependent and interdependent on others for survival, satisfaction and success.

By the way, independence should not be confused with self-reliance. It is a sign of maturity to be able to stand alone at times and not to worry about what others think of you. This is self-reliance. However putting your energy into standing alone and pushing others away when you could be far more creative and contributive by working in with other people is just foolish pride.

The poet John Donne wrote those oft-quoted words; "No man is an island unto himself." We could also say that no business is an island unto itself, especially today with outsourcing and specialisation on the increase. At the end of the day the franchisor and franchisee are interdependent. The sooner both parties realise this the more likely they are to maturely address issues of concern in a direct and open manner.

The myth of subservience

Despite what a franchise agreement sets down about franchisees having to do what the franchisor states, the fact is that the franchisee is responsible for running their own business. He or she is not an employee of the franchisor. It is vital that franchisors always keep in mind that the franchise relationship is in no way an employer/ employee situation. In fact, for many new franchisees, one of the most important and exciting aspects of being in a franchise is the prospect of being self-employed.

Franchisors who have converted company owned stores to franchised outlets often run into initial problems with this issue. The psychological shift in attitude from owning a store to owning the intellectual property rights under which the store operates is subtle, yet significant. A franchisee will naturally be possessive about his or her new store and will react aggressively if the franchisor is perceived to be moving in on their personal space or territory.

The franchisor also can't simply sack a franchisee if he or she doesn't toe the line or if they don't perform. Terminating a franchise agreement is a lot more complex and costly than terminating the services of an employee. Franchisees are usually employers themselves and have their own employee hassles to worry about. They appreciate being treated with the respect of employers in their own right.

Franchisors who try to run their system using an authoritarian approach may find themselves in for a rude shock. While the franchisor might hold a position of power and strength over many aspects of how their system operates, this does not mean that the franchisee should be subservient to the franchisor's wishes.

The myth of equal power

There is another issue related to this. It concerns whether the relationship between a franchisor and a franchisee should be equal if it is to be fair.

Decisions need to be made every day concerning how a franchise system operates and the responsibility for many of these decisions sits with the franchisor. It is a fact of franchising life that the franchisor holds more power than the franchisee. After all it is the franchisor's intellectual property which is often at stake.

In my experience it is both impractical and undesirable for franchisees to have an equal say in all decisions concerning the running of a franchise network.

The question of what is fair is, of course, an important issue and franchisors need to be careful that they do not contravene local laws that define unfair or harsh and oppressive conduct. However it is a myth to think that franchise relationships should be equal if they are to be fair.

This issue of leadership and who should have the power to make decisions is discussed in greater depth in Chapter 10.

The myth of franchisee compliance

At this point I want to briefly introduce an issue related to franchisee suitability (which we will take up in more detail in Chapters 7 and 16). Most franchisors, in the early stages of developing their systems, will have had some unpleasant experiences with unhappy or disruptive franchisees. The franchisor can then assume that people who are too lively or independent (such as those with whom they clashed) will always be a problem and that they should therefore be looking for compliant, subservient franchisees who will just do what they are told.

The truth might be that relationship difficulties in the early stages were largely due to teething problems in the system and the inability and inexperience of franchisor staff to deal with emotionally charged issues. Conflict often occurs when difficulties arise between two parties who are insecure or unsure of what they are doing.

As the franchisor gets its act together and builds its 'corporate confidence', it will be in a far better position to handle difficult situations. Franchisees who may have been labelled as trouble makers earlier on may now be seen as dynamic, motivated people who, while needing to be handled sensitively, are high achievers who help to keep the system responsive to change. In fact our research shows that the most profitable and contributive franchisees are entrepreneurial people with the urge to continually be better, faster and smarter than their competitors.

So rather than just looking for people who will be highly compliant and follow the rules, franchisors need to realise that if their system is to develop they need high achievers — people who will test the boundaries of the system occasionally, but will also play by the rules if these are spelt out clearly. Again, to manage these people the relationship needs to be firm but fair and not too personal.

The myth of system infallibility

Most franchise concepts have been built on a specialised product or service combined with a successful business system. The founders of these concepts will have inevitably developed their systems through trial and error and have probably made just about every mistake that could be made. In a sense this accumulated experience and wisdom is what you are paying for when you buy a franchise.

However a system is only good as long as it fits the needs of the environment in which it operates. A fact of life is that things change — markets change, customer preferences and needs change, employee expectations change. It is therefore a myth to think that a system that works like magic will always do so.

So if you are a franchisor, don't be so arrogant and narrow minded to think that your system is infallible and must never be questioned. And when franchisees do raise questions over aspects of your system (as they inevitably will), before you come down too hard, check to see if their ideas have merit. Franchising is a business — it's not a religion.

The 40% factor

Another aspect of the system infallibility myth is to do with how much the system actually contributes to a business' success. We need to keep in mind that people run systems, systems don't run people. This is often demonstrated when we compare the performance of company run operations with franchised operations or when a franchise changes hands. Let's look further at these two scenarios.

Despite the belief in the magnificence of their systems, many franchisors fail dismally when they attempt to convert franchised operations to company owned. What they discover is that their systems are not sophisticated enough to successfully drive the business. The enthusiasm and commitment of the franchisee must never be underestimated in the success of a franchise.

This was also brought home to me when, as a franchisor, I had four franchised stores that were under performing so badly that I was under pressure from various sources to either close them down or de-brand them. Yet my instincts told me that these were all good sites. Over a period of a year as we systematically found new franchisees for these stores, sales immediately improved significantly. In one store, sales doubled within twelve months. Same site, same equipment, same brand, same systems, same everything — except the people. The actual figures for these changeovers are shown in the chart overleaf. The dotted circles indicate the dates of change in ownership.

Through this and other research I have concluded that an individual franchisee contributes an average of 40% to the success of a particular business. The systems, site and brand contribute the rest.

The impact of a new franchisee on sales
(graph shows quarterly sales figures)

The myth of the franchisee customer

Although franchisees may pay money in the form of franchise fees to receive support and services from their franchisor, they are not really customers in the true sense of the word, ie. one who purchases goods from another. It can in fact prove to be unhealthy for a franchisor to encourage a customer-supplier relationship with its franchisees.

In the open market for services, customers and suppliers are free to deal with whom they choose, when they choose. Suppliers also have to compete for business by demonstrating the value of their services. Franchisors, however, do not compete with other groups to provide the franchise package of services to their franchisees. These services should be guided by the terms of the franchise agreement and common sense.

Of course, a good franchisor will provide the highest quality support services for its franchisees to ensure their profitability and satisfaction. The best franchisor companies in the world are in fact extremely service focussed and build this into their organisational culture. They recognise that they are a service organisation. However it is unwise to confuse a customer-supplier relationship with a service oriented relationship. One is a part of the other but they are not the same thing.

Ultimately, the franchisees do not dictate the terms of the services provided by the franchisor, although in a healthy relationship, modifications will be negotiated from time to time. The discipline and integrity of a franchise network depends heavily on franchisees accepting that they must follow the rules and guidelines of the franchisor, as defined in their formal contract.

It is when the formal nature of the relationship becomes confused that power struggles are more likely to occur. For instance, a franchisee might threaten to take their business elsewhere if they are unhappy with the services they are receiving from their franchisor — a hollow threat (given the nature of most franchise agreements) which is likely to undermine the relationship.

The exception to the rule — franchisor as supplier

There can be situations where a franchisor does in fact become a supplier of goods to franchisees. Many relationship problems involve the franchisor taking on such a formal supplier role by selling goods to franchisees through warehousing arrangements, especially if products are not available from other sources.

This can create a feeling that the franchisor is 'double dipping' in terms of royalties and gross profit mark-ups. While franchisees may still be receiving good commercial value with competitive prices under such an arrangement, it often leads to a souring of the relationship.

The saying that I referred to earlier "When perception meets reality, reality comes off second best", is particularly relevant here. Although franchisees may be receiving good value under a supply arrangement, if they perceive that the arrangement is unfair they will behave as though it is unfair, usually with hostility.

Franchisors need to be very careful in setting themselves up as suppliers to their franchisees. I recommend they draw a clear distinction between their role as supplier and franchisor. For instance, it can be useful to have a separate management team looking after the needs of franchisees in the two areas.

Franchisors should always have a well thought out strategic reason for becoming a supplier and this should be regularly reviewed. Times change and what may be useful at one time may no longer be feasible or advisable if market conditions change. It is also advisable to communicate relevant aspects of the strategy to franchisees in a factual manner, rather than feel it has to be a big secret. When people don't have the facts they tend to fill in the blanks with whatever information comes their way, which is usually distorted at best.

Franchisees need to be careful not to be too quick to judge a franchisor that supplies them products. Franchisors will have often invested significant capital and resources to set up a suitable manufacturing and/or distribution company. It is unreasonable to expect them to operate this as a charity. They are entitled to receive a fair and reasonable commercial return. Furthermore, running a franchise company is not as profitable as many people imagine.

The most useful approach here is for franchisees and franchisors to stick to the facts and not get caught up in taking moral stands. The point to always return to is whether franchisees are receiving a quality product and good service at competitive prices, or not. In some countries and states, local legislation may override the terms in a franchise agreement that compels franchisees to buy specific products from their franchisor, providing all the more reason for franchisors to ensure their supply arrangements are competitive.

In the next chapter we will continue our discussion on common myths and mistaken assumptions that occur in franchise networks.

In summary

There are several common myths about the franchise relationship that, if left unchallenged, can leave people vulnerable to frustration and disappointment. It pays for franchisors and franchisees to regularly check their assumptions and to modify their expectations of each other if these are unrealistic.

Action Tips:

- Embrace the fact that much of your success and happiness in life will come from establishing interdependent relationships with others. Actively seek to establish such relationships.

- Ask for help and support when you need it and be prepared to share your knowledge and resources with others.

- Don't confuse self-reliance — the ability to stand for what you believe in — with independence or foolish pride.

- Seek and encourage competent, enterprising franchisees to join your franchise network and be sure you have good systems within which they can work. 40% of your system's success depends on the calibre of franchisees.

- Set up processes for continually improving your franchise system. It's a business, not dogma set in stone.

- Remain focussed on delivering great service to all the people who depend on you for something. However resist the temptation of creating your franchisee/franchisor relationship around a customer-supplier mind-set.

- If the franchisor is a supplier of goods, be sure that supply arrangements are strategically and commercially sound, transparent and competitive.

- If you are a franchisor, treat your franchisees as independent business people with whom you have a business partnership.

- If you are a franchisee, accept that it's okay for you not to have the same level of power as your franchisor on issues of strategy and policy. It's just the way things are in a franchise system.

CHAPTER FIVE
The Friendship Trap

In an attempt to build strong relationships with their franchisees, some franchisors feel they should become friends with their franchisees. I believe that this is not a good idea and franchisors who take this approach can place themselves or their franchisees in an embarrassing situation when tough decisions need to be made.

Friendship and friendly are not the same

The franchise relationship is first and foremost a commercial relationship. As such, from time to time commercial decisions will need to be made, or issues raised by one party that may create discomfort for the other. For instance, a franchisor may need to ask a franchisee to remove unauthorised products from their store, or a franchisee may need to raise issues concerning the competence of a field manager with the franchisor. In such cases the relationship may become strained for a time until the reasons for the decision are fully understood.

Friendships can cloud these important issues or prevent them being addressed, leading to inappropriate compromises or problems being swept under the carpet. I have also seen cases where franchisors have had personal (and often irrelevant) information used against them when difficult decisions needed to be made.

I am not suggesting here that business relationships should not be cordial and friendly. Indeed healthy business relationships often involve some frivolity and fun. However, do not confuse friendly relationships with close friendships. If you have built a close friendship with a franchisee or your franchisor I suggest you agree that, when business issues need to be discussed, a professional and businesslike approach is maintained.

The CEO who lost his Mercedes

One of my early consulting clients was the CEO of a growing franchisor company. For years he had dreamed of owning a Mercedes Benz. In the first three years of establishing the business he created close and personal relationships with his franchisees and would often boast to me how they were all one big, happy family.

When he reached his first milestone of thirty five stores he bought a gleaming white, top of the range, E-series Mercedes with leather upholstery. Yet his dream turned to a nightmare when he found himself continually facing wise cracks from his franchisee 'family' about how they were funding his opulent lifestyle every time he made a decision they did not like.

He subsequently traded in his white pride and joy for a Ford station wagon and despite continuing to grow this profitable business, he gradually became more and more cynical and disillusioned about his future in franchising. Eventually to the shock of his franchisees, he sold the business to an astute investor who, among other things, has kept his relationships at a professional level and is still running this profitable business twelve years on.

Franchisees as business partners

Organisational culture is a powerful influence on people's behaviour and relationships. An organisation's true culture can be seen by the way people talk and behave when they are at work, especially when they are under pressure. (This should not be confused with the espoused culture that is written in the corporate brochures or presented in formal speeches.)

Whether they realise it or not, leaders of franchise organisations have a tremendous influence over the culture of their franchise system. In particular they need to be careful about the way they talk about their franchisees when they are with their management teams and the way they relate to franchisees when sensitive issues are at stake.

If a franchisor believes its franchisees are cogs in its empire, the franchisees will most probably behave accordingly, mechanically following the system. But it is unlikely they will show much initiative, enthusiasm or creativity. Cogs just do what they are programmed to do.

However, if the franchisor treats its franchisees with the respect of fellow business people who are in business to make a profit, a different story unfolds. Franchisees who are stimulated and challenged by discussions about profitability, cash flow, marketing strategies and sales targets will be more likely to respond like switched on business people — to seize opportunities in their local market and aim at being the best they can be.

So the most effective way to educate franchisees to think and behave like successful business people is to treat them as such — as business partners who are working with their franchisor to achieve profitability and mutual success. The following research demonstrates the power of our expectations and prejudices on other people.

The Pygmalion Effect

When I was completing my masters degree in education I came across some rather profound research on how teacher attitudes can affect student performance.

In a study by two educational psychologists, Rosenthal and Jacobsen, primary school teachers were given false information about the new pupils in their class. They were told that some pupils were highly intelligent and responsive while others were dull and distracted. In reality there was no difference between the two groups — the students had been randomly assigned to one of the groups. Yet, at the end of the year the 'bright' students consistently outperformed the 'dull' students on a range of measures. The teachers also rated the bright students as being more pleasant to work with.

Although the teachers in the study claimed that they treated both groups the same, they had subconsciously turned their expectations and prejudices into reality. Bright students became bright students and dull students became dull students. Rosenthal and Jacobsen named this phenomenon 'The Pygmalion Effect' after George Bernard Shaw's famous play about a professor who transforms a rough, uneducated street girl into an impressive, highly refined lady. The transformation largely takes place through the power of the professor's belief in the girl's potential. (Pygmalion was actually a sculptor and King of Cypress who fell in love with an ivory statue which he had made and which came to life in answer to his prayer.)

The Pygmalion Effect has clear implications for anyone who manages or coaches other people. Never underestimate the power of your attitudes on the people who look to you for leadership, guidance and support.

The road to hell is paved with good intentions

The founders of successful franchise companies are often visionary people with a strong commitment to their concept, product or service. They are not just motivated by money. They are excited by the idea of developing their ideas further and sharing their expertise with others who will join them in their mission to expand the market. The idea of helping others to be successful can be a very strong motivation for these people.

As this success materialises, franchisor-founders can assume that, because they have a good relationship with their franchisees, and have helped them to be successful, the franchisees will always "do the right thing by them". For example they will always pay their correct royalty fees, attend all meetings, follow the system and only sell the authorised range of products.

Because of the franchisor's strong emotional investment in their system, they might expect everyone else to share this enthusiasm. Yet, as we will see in later chapters, un-met expectations are often a source of disappointment and conflict on both sides.

The fact is that on many issues, people operate from different positions with different agendas and different interests. Assumptions that the franchisee will always operate from the same perspective as the franchisor are thus flawed.

Cognitive Dissonance

While I am a believer in the inherent goodness of people, I also try to moderate this with realism. As was discussed earlier, perception is a powerful motivating force and people will often rationalise their behaviour by changing their perception of events.

For instance, there will be a certain percentage of staff in any establishment who will steal money if circumstances create a tempting environment. These people may then rationalise their behaviour by saying things like "the boss was ripping me off with low wages so I was only doing the fair thing by taking the money back". Or, "The boss is making so much money that she won't mind a few dollars missing here and there".

This rationalising behaviour occurs because of a phenomenon technically known as 'cognitive dissonance' and people fall under its spell every day in all sorts of ways. Cognitive dissonance refers to the uncomfortable feelings that come from behaving or thinking in a way which may be in conflict with previously held beliefs.

Instead of changing our behaviour to reduce the dissonance, we change our cognition or the way we think about the event. In this way we try to bring our uncomfortable feelings under control.

For instance, a business owner who is having cash flow problems may rationalise not paying her creditors by thinking "It is good for me to keep them waiting. It will do them good. After all their service is often slack and this will be a message to them". Thus she doesn't feel so bad about holding back cheques to suppliers.

Or a manager who made a key decision that turned out badly may blame his staff. Although he was responsible he may shift the blame by thinking, "If they had provided me with better information I would have decided differently on this one". And so he retains his own sense of competence — after all it was their fault!

People often think differently about the same issues

We cannot afford to be naive to the realities of human nature. To assume that franchisees and franchisors will think the same about issues to do with what is right and proper for a franchise network is to ignore basic human psychology.

Franchisees face their own unique pressures and their view of the world will often be different from that of the franchisor. For instance, a franchisor who believes that franchisees will only stock authorised products and will always follow the system because it works well, are ignoring the franchisee's belief that they should be able to do whatever their customers ask or what might bring them a sale.

Franchisors should try to look at things from the franchisee's point of view. In order to run a successful business the franchisee needs to get right into the thick of things. They have to be in there serving customers, working alongside staff, maintaining standards, controlling suppliers and generally having their finger on the pulse of the business. There is no getting around this.

When a franchisee takes a hands-on approach to the business it is unlikely they will see the big picture. This requires an objective attitude, information from a range of sources, and time to think and plan. It is the franchisor's responsibility to keep sight of this big picture. It is unrealistic to expect franchisees to also share the larger strategic perspective.

An individual franchisee who makes decisions from time to time which are not in the best interests of the franchisor or the larger group, is most probably operating from the only view he has of the business at the time — a short-term one. This usually means the weekly sales figures.

Many so-called deviations from the franchisor's concept are not deliberate or malicious acts of rebellion. Such decisions may be made with good intentions, however misguided these might appear from the total network perspective.

We opened this chapter with the question — "Should franchisees and franchisors be friends?" Rather than a simple yes or no the answer is more like yes *and* no. Be friendly and respectful in your relationships with others, but be warned. The human ego plays tricks on us all from time to time. If you choose to combine a close friendship with a franchise relationship be prepared to have your friendship tested.

In summary

The interdependent nature of their relationship means that franchisees and franchisors can have a strong influence over each other. However there are also a number of pitfalls if the relationship becomes too close and personal. Understanding some of the basic laws of human motivation such as Cognitive Dissonance and the Pygmalion Effect can help both parties to better manage their close interpersonal relationships.

Action Tips:

- Maintain a friendly but professional relationship with your franchisees or franchisor.

- When differences of opinion arise, keep discussions within relevant boundaries, ie. don't allow personal prejudices to cloud commercial facts.

- If you want to create a close, warm family culture in your franchise system you need to accept that most families also have a dysfunctional side to them!

- Pay careful attention to how you talk about other people behind closed doors and how you behave under pressure. This is the real test of your corporate culture and values.

- Harness the power of the Pygmalion Effect. Bring out the best in others by showing them you have confidence in their abilities.

- Invest in good systems for maintaining financial and management controls and define these clearly and unambiguously. Do not leave important compliance issues to people's individual judgement.

CHAPTER SIX

What Franchising Can Learn from Marriage

In the first part of this book we learned that there are good commercial reasons for maintaining healthy franchise relationships. For instance, they encourage the sharing of knowledge and resources which are so important in gaining and sustaining a competitive edge.

We also learned that franchising is in many ways similar to other interdependent relationships such as marriage, where two parties depend on each other for mutual satisfaction and support. The feelings of excitement and hope for a happy and prosperous future experienced in the early stages of the franchise relationship are not dissimilar to those experienced by people embarking on a partnership at the personal level.

Research findings

Most of us have had first hand knowledge of how challenging relationships can be. For instance, when our partner behaves in certain ways we may feel our tolerance and patience are being tested to the limit. (Not surprisingly, we probably fail to consider at these times that *our* behaviour may also be affecting our partner in similar ways!)

While reviewing the research literature on interdependent relationships such as marriage I discovered some remarkable lessons for the franchising sector from the work of one of my psychology teachers. Professor Kim Halford from the University of Queensland reviewed hundreds of studies on marriage and partnership breakdowns to identify any consistent principles or trends.

His research showed that during the first year, half of all married people have some doubts about their decision and wonder whether the relationship is going to work out. Of this half, 20 per cent experience relationship problems. In other words, 10 per cent of legally committed relationships develop problems reasonably quickly.

This figure is similar to my own research findings that, at any one time, around 10% of franchisees will feel they have issues with their franchisor that they would like to see resolved. Naturally these figures will differ depending on the conflict resolution systems a franchisor has in place and the business challenges a particular franchise system may be facing. (Business and financial pressures inevitably exacerbate conflict.)

The most fascinating and important aspect of the marriage research is that the couples that were going to experience serious problems could be predicted in advance with **91 per cent accuracy,** using the following four predictive indicators. You will see that they have great relevance to franchising.

1. An inability to deal with conflict

2. Poor communication skills

3. Unrealistic expectations

4. A lack of supportive networks

Let's look at each of these more closely.

1. An inability to deal constructively with conflict

The single best predictor of partnership distress is the poor management of conflict. The worse a person's conflict management skills, the more likely they are to end up in a partnership breakdown.

The most important skill in managing conflict is the ability of each party to listen and show interest and respect for the other's point of view. Skills to do with active listening and assertiveness are extremely useful here.

Another important skill in managing conflict is simply talking about the problem. Numerous studies show that partners who avoid talking about topics that they are in conflict over inevitably suffer from relationship problems. The message here is that withdrawing attention, changing the topic or avoiding a person with whom you are in conflict will not solve the problem. In fact in an interdependent relationship it will only make things worse.

At the other extreme, attacking the other party is just as bad. This actually leads to an escalation of hostility. In business we see this escalation of hostility played out through litigation battles every day.

If there was one skill which all franchisors and franchisees should be trained in as part of their business management, it should be how to deal with conflict. There are always going to be times when one or both parties perceive that their needs are not being adequately met. Franchisors, in particular, need to accept that the management of conflict comes with the job. Chapter 9 provides many practical tips on how to resolve conflict sensibly.

2. Poor communication skills

If communication is poor, the chances of conflict and partnership breakdowns are high. Good communication is simply the ability to make yourself understood or to understand others. Although it sounds easy, most people have great difficulty being listened to and listening to others. Here are a few of the most common blocks to good communication.

Differences in interpretation

One of the best definitions of communication I have heard is by social researcher, Hugh Mackay, who says, "It's not what our message does to the listener but what the listener does with our message that determines our success as communicators". In other words it is not so much what we say that is important but the meaning that other people attribute to our message that counts.

People will often interpret things differently from what you intended. So it pays to check the message by asking people to put into their own words what has been agreed on.

Sending double messages

If you are not clear on what you are saying this will probably come across in your voice and body language. As a result the other person gets a mixed message. Think about what you really want to say and, if you do not yet feel prepared, delay the discussion until you have had time to prepare your thoughts. Write down the outcome you want to see as a result of your conversation and then ensure your message is consistent with this.

Being aggressive or submissive

As mentioned earlier, being pushy and domineering is just as bad as avoiding issues or trying to appease everyone. Both approaches turn people off and inevitably leave issues unresolved. A direct approach is best, while being respectful of your own and the other person's feelings and interests.

Our feelings get in the way

Strong feelings can influence almost the entire meaning of what we say to another person, regardless of the words we use. If you are angry or upset about an issue, leave discussing it to a later time when you feel clearer and more objective. Don't let your impatience or frustration rule your behaviour. A more controlled and patient approach will definitely yield more effective results.

3. Unrealistic expectations

Unrealistic expectations at the start of a relationship are highly correlated with feelings of subsequent disappointment and betrayal. Unrealistic expectations can come from many sources in the franchise relationship. Both franchisees and franchisors can suffer from shattered expectations even though these have not always been intentionally created.

The franchise sales and qualification period is absolutely the best time for clarifying the expectations of both parties. The franchisor should have a checklist of questions to test the franchisee's expectations and the franchisee should be encouraged to use a list of pre-prepared questions in discussions with the franchisor such as those listed in some of the better Franchisee Guides available on the market.

With regard to the operational aspects of the business, the simplest and most effective way to communicate what is involved is to have potential franchisees work in an existing franchised business for a few days. Nothing communicates better than first hand experience.

Because unrealistic expectations are common in franchising, the next chapter is devoted entirely to this topic.

4. Lack of supportive networks

The final predictor of partnership breakdowns is concerned with the level of outside support the parties receive. In a personal relationship this might relate to friends or family who are supportive of the individual partners and their relationship. In practice this means that when problems occur, there is someone to talk to who will not undermine the relationship.

This principle is very appropriate to franchising and can be creatively applied to both franchisors and franchisees. Many franchisors report that they gain great support and encouragement from networking with their peers over problems which arise in their networks.

Franchisees should also be encouraged to mix with each other so they can provide mutual support and advice on how to deal with any problems which might arise with the franchisor. Some franchise groups also use the services of an objective but supportive mediator or facilitator to listen to problems either party might be having in the franchise relationship.

The most important principle here is that the outside support person should have honourable intentions and be favourably disposed to the idea of franchising and the existing relationship. For instance, if either party sought outside advice from a person who wanted to undermine the relationship this would exacerbate the problems rather than resolve them. Unfortunately, legal advisers, through their adversarial training, often fill this negative role. There have also been cases of unscrupulous lawyers or consultants who have deliberately sought to create conflict and dissatisfaction within franchise groups for their own short-term gain.

It takes two to Tango

Take serious note of these factors. If you and your prospective franchisee or franchisor are having difficulties understanding each other prior to finalising the signing of a franchise agreement, chances are that this communication problem will only get worse, not better. In such a case it would be timely to discuss where the communication problem seems to lie and what both parties might do to improve it.

Also of relevance is that all four predictors are interactive behaviours. In other words it takes two to Tango. You may be tempted to blame a communication problem on the personality of the other person. A more productive route might be to take a good long look at your own habits of communication and dealing with conflict, as well as the expectations you have and the type of outside input you are receiving.

Lessons from these four factors

Looking at the positive side of these four factors we could say that good long-term relationships can be enhanced by using the following common sense approaches.

Learn how to deal with conflict

Franchisees and franchisors need to have sound conflict resolution skills. If these are lacking, training should be provided in these skills in the early stages of the relationship. It is a good idea to include some sort of assessment of a person's ability to resolve conflict as part of selecting both franchisor staff and franchisees.

Practise your listening skills

For the entrepreneurial person who is creative, action oriented and task focussed (as many franchisors and franchisees are) taking time to understand another person's thoughts, feelings and experience can be seen as a distraction from 'getting on with things'. This attitude can be an excuse for avoiding issues, or a way of protecting our own pet ideas. After all, not listening to others means we don't have to accommodate their thoughts into our plans, they can't criticise us and we can continue to work in the way that gives us the most satisfaction. Chapter 9 elaborates on how to avoid these blind spots.

Check your expectations

Franchisees and franchisors should systematically verify each other's expectations through the use of checklists and discussions. Both parties need to spell out their understanding of what the other has previously communicated in key areas.

Seek advisers who have your best interests at heart

Seek out peers, mentors and advisers who are supportive of the franchise relationship and who can act as an objective sounding board on issues that you may not yet be ready to discuss with your franchisee or franchisor. Beware of people who make money from the creation of conflict.

In summary

Breakdowns in interdependent relationships can be predicted by looking at the expectations of the parties, the type of outside advice and support they are receiving, their communication skills and their ability to deal with conflict.

Action Tips:

- Talk through your differences with others making sure you listen to their views with respect. Avoiding a person you are in conflict with will never solve the problem.

- Assess people's ability to handle conflict before accepting them for management or franchisee roles.

- Incorporate conflict resolution into your training programs.

- When making important agreements check that your message has been understood by asking the other person to put it into their own words.

- Delay sensitive discussions until you have prepared your thoughts on what you want to say.

- Do not engage in discussions when you are feeling emotional or angry.

- Treat misunderstandings prior to the signing of a franchise agreement as an early warning sign and raise it for discussion.

- Use structured checklists to verify franchisee and franchisor expectations of each other. After important discussions recap on what has been said or agreed to.

- Build supportive networks with positive peers who you can use as a sounding board when necessary.

- Build a relationship with one or more facilitators or mediators you can call on if you need help to resolve communication problems.

- Do not accept advice from people who are prejudiced against the franchise relationship or have a vested interest in the creation of conflict.

CHAPTER SEVEN
Great Expectations

As we learned in Chapter 6 the most common reason why difficulties occur in interdependent relationships is that the expectations of one or both parties were not met. In this chapter we will identify the areas where expectations are often out of alignment. We will also cover the practical things everyone can do to check if a franchisee is really suitable and prepared to enter into a franchise relationship.

When perception meets reality

Because expectations and assumptions exist in a person's mind, they can be difficult to manage. What makes this especially difficult is that people tend to have different perceptions of events and situations depending on their perspective. Whatever the facts may be in a situation, a person will behave according to the information he or she has available to them at the time.

Remember the wise words from Dr Bob Dick, **"When perception meets reality, reality comes out second best"**.

The problem of differing perceptions and expectations can largely be prevented in the early stages of the franchise relationship if everyone keeps discussions very specific and writes things down. This enables both parties to review information together, and minimises the chances of misunderstandings.

However despite good intentions on the part of both sides, there is typically a lot happening and a lot of information to absorb at this time. It is thus advisable to never assume anything. As the saying goes — to assume makes an **ASS** out of **U** and **ME**.

In Chapter 2 we reviewed the different roles of the franchisee and franchisor. Because each party brings a different perspective to the relationship there is a big chance that the expectations and perceptions of each will be different — even in the same situation. So let's look more closely at these differences in perspective.

The franchisee's perspective

Franchisees typically have a high financial **and** emotional invest-ment in the success of their business. For instance, in establish-ing the franchise, they will often have invested their life savings or borrowed against their homes. Not only is their financial security dependent on the success of the business, but so is their pride. They will want to be seen by their friends and family as an astute, competent and successful business person. This means they will tend to be reluctant to take risks unless they are sure the risk will pay off.

As the person who is usually responsible for the day to day running of the business the franchisee will also tend to have strong views on how to best service the **local** needs of their customers.

Another key issue for the franchisee is that they will probably have bought the business with an expectation that they will have a reasonable amount of autonomy as to how they do things. And as it is *their* business there may be a reluctance to share what they see as sensitive financial information with the franchisor.

Finally, as the franchisee gains more confidence in their busi-ness they will tend to become more independent and likely to want to develop their own way of doing things. This is particularly so of franchisees who are more entrepreneurial by nature.

The franchisor's perspective

Compare this with the franchisor's perspective.

If the founder of the company is still involved in the business he or she will typically be a visionary entrepreneur who is motivated by the prospect of building a large, successful franchise network. As the entrepreneurial spirit is typically competitive and dominant by nature, entrepreneurs are often impatient and demanding. Where there is a difference of opinion, they can be pushy in getting their own way. They sometimes fail to appreciate that a franchisee may be reluctant to invest in a new idea that is not yet totally proven.

If a large corporation owns the franchise network the CEO is likely to be driving the group toward the achievement of ambitious strategic goals. So decisions will still tend to be driven from the top down.

As the strategist with the big picture perspective, the franchisor will also tend to take a broad long-term view of marketing issues. This may not meet the short-term local needs of a franchisee.

Because of the importance of maintaining the reputation and values of the brand, the franchisor will want strict compliance to operating and customer service standards. As mentioned above the franchisee may have different priorities or a different view on how to service their local customers.

Finally, most franchisors want to receive regular and accurate financial and management information on the performance of all franchises so that benchmarking and continuous improvement goals can be set. Franchisees may be reluctant to share such information feeling it is an invasion of their privacy.

These differences in perspective are summarised below. They inevitably create tensions between the parties at different times.

Franchisor's perspective	Franchisee's perspective
Entrepreneurial, impatient, "let's do it"	More cautious with risk, "let's wait" and see"
Wants to make decisions and have them implemented by the network	Wants to have a say in decisions that impact on them
Takes a national perspective on customer needs	Takes a local perspective on customer needs
Focussed on long term outcomes and strategic issues	Focussed on weekly sales outcomes and day to day operational issues
Wants consistency and compliance to the system	Wants some autonomy and flexibility in how they do things
Wants open sharing of financial and business information	Can be reluctant to share financial and business information

Feeling misled

In addition to the different perspectives identified above there tends to be six common areas where expectations between franchisees and franchisors can become out of alignment. Where this misalignment is significant in the mind of one party it can lead to feelings of being misled and a subsequent breakdown of trust.

After examining these six areas we will look at some specific things franchisees and franchisors can do to align their expectations and reduce the likelihood of problems in these areas.

1. The level and type of support

A franchisee may believe they are going to get a higher level of training or support than is realistic from the franchisor's point of view.
They may then feel betrayed or angry because they are expected to
take full responsibility for the performance of the business.

For instance, franchisees may expect help with staff selection
and training, assistance with the day to day operations of the business or the provision of emergency back up staff. The franchisor
on the other hand may be adamant that their role is to provide
the systems for the franchisee to manage these functions and that
they are definitely not in the business of organising the franchisee's
operations or staffing.

As a franchisee I remember feeling extremely aggrieved at
3.00am one morning because my field manager would not come
to my store and bake with me when my baker phoned in sick. I just
couldn't accept his (reasonable) reply that his job was not to bake
in my store and it was my responsibility to manage my own staffing
problems.

2. Financial return on effort

A franchisee may believe that the profit he or she is earning from
the business is inadequate given the initial investment and the
hours they are working. The franchisor may however claim this is a
satisfactory or perhaps even an excellent return.

The problem here is that each party has a different definition of
what profit includes and is thus operating from different assumptions. For instance the franchisor may regard the franchisee's
wages, interest repayments and extra benefits such as a car or holidays as profit while the franchisee sees profit as what is left after *all*
expenses are paid.

Franchisees can also become disillusioned with the fees and
expenses they are paying, feeling these are unfairly eroding profit.
(This is covered in detail in Chapter 8 when we discuss 'The
Franchise E-Factor'). If the franchisor is supplying products or
corporate items such as stationery or uniforms the pricing of these
items may become a bone of contention.

Working capital and cash flow also commonly emerge as problem
areas. Before starting the business a franchisee may say that working
capital is no problem. However if it is never clearly defined how
much working capital is needed and what it will be needed for,

slow initial sales can cause problems. A common scenario is that the franchisee assumes their business will be profitable from day one and that working capital was only needed for the purchase of stock. Because they have no reserves they request that royalty fees be waived so they can draw a wage. The franchisor is then placed in a difficult situation because they felt they made it clear the franchisee may have to initially support him or herself using the reserves of working capital. A stand off can then occur.

3. Small business lifestyle

There is a certain glamour associated with the idea of being your own boss and working for yourself. Franchisees that have not been in business before or who have not had direct family contact with a small business may be naive to the reality of working long hours six or seven days a week as well as the ongoing pressures and uncertainty of the small business lifestyle.

This is particularly so if they have a romanticised view of what running the franchise will be like or if the franchisee has not had an opportunity to actually work in this type of franchised business prior to starting out on their own.

Franchisees in one retail group that I worked with found themselves working seven days a week when trading hours were extended. They banded together demanding their franchisor assist them with relief staffing because the franchise sales brochure had clearly stated that the business would enhance their lifestyle and allow them to spend more time with their family!

4. Level of consultation

Franchisors regularly talk about wanting to empower franchisees to have more say in the running of the franchise system. However there is often confusion over what this means in practice.

We need to understand the difference between consultative and participative decision making. In the former, the franchisor listens to the views and ideas of franchisees, then makes its own decision. In the latter, franchisees have an equal say in the decision making process.

If franchisees believe they are involved in the final decision making process whereas they are just being consulted, they will tend to become frustrated and annoyed, believing they have been misled. (Chapter 10 covers this important issue of decision making in a franchise system in greater detail.)

5. Sense of community

The promise of being in business 'for yourself but not by yourself' implies ongoing contact with other people. However this will largely depend on the location of the franchise territory and the number of forums and meetings that are organised. Some franchisees find they are having little contact with other people and thus experience feelings of isolation and disappointment.

Given that one of the most powerful of all human needs is to have a sense of belonging, feelings of isolation can be a significant source of discontent.

6. The obligations of each party

In a fast growing network franchisor staff will tend to be wearing several 'hats' in order to fulfil the company's obligations within budgetary constraints. In the midst of all this activity franchisees will be gaining more confidence in the operation of their businesses. They will thus tend to become more demanding about what they are receiving for their royalty fees and more discerning regarding the type of support they expect from their franchisor.

Franchisors can sometimes react to these demands by throwing more services and more activities at franchisees, feeling they have to justify themselves and their fees. This can lead to confusion over the obligations of both parties.

Questions to consider

Before entering into a franchise relationship I suggest you consider the 15 questions listed on pages 64-65. Our research shows that these are the areas where people can get themselves into trouble.

Here are some other tips for franchisees.

Before you buy into a franchise:

• Be sure to complete thorough profitability and cash flow projections on the business. Have these checked by someone with good business skills and ensure they are based on sound assumptions.

Although you may wish the franchisor to review these with you, understand that, for legal reasons, they will be reluctant to make representations on sales or profits. The franchisor may however be prepared to provide you with some objective financial models they have developed from existing franchises.

Questions for Franchisees to Consider

Ask yourself this...	And consider this ...
Are you clear on why you want to go into this business? Will the business satisfy this need?	• Just looking to buy a job is not a strong enough reason. • if you are very ambitious there may be limits on what you can achieve with the one franchise.
Would you be happy to work in this business for long periods at a time without a break?	• You may need to work 6 or 7 days a week or for long hours. • when things go wrong you can't expect your franchisor to sort it out for you.
Are you proud to tell people that you will be running this business?	• Consider how you will feel when people ask you what you do for a living. • Being a franchisee with this brand will become a large part of your identity.
How does your family feel about you going into this business?	• If your family expects you to put time and energy into other priorities tension will be inevitable.
What is your gut feel about the people who own or run the franchisor company?	• You are signing an agreement to work with these people for 5 or 10 years. • If you are not comfortable with the culture or the way things are done conflict is inevitable.
Are you comfortable selling to customers and networking with new people to promote your business?	• Nothing happens until somebody sells something. • If you are not prepared to go out and sell your products or services it is unlikely that you can lead others to do so.
Are you happy to participate in forums and group activities, which could involve travel away from home?	• You will be expected to participate in ongoing training and business forums.
Are you happy to invest the money and time to continually learn new knowledge and skills?	• If you don't keep developing professionally, you and your business will get stale.
When you disagree with someone something you feel strongly about, can you talk it through without exploding or giving up?	• Some conflict will be inevitable. about • If you are used to getting your way by sulking or becoming aggressive or vindictive you will end up with serious problems with your franchisor.

Ask yourself this...	And consider this...
Can you cope with stressful events and financial pressure?	• Things are bound to happen which are unexpected and beyond your control. • Some of these events may place you or the business under significant strain.
Can you supervise and motivate other people?	• If your business involves staff they must be managed and motivated. • You will never succeed without high performing staff.
Are you happy sharing your business information with other people?	• Most franchisors require full disclosure of financial and business information on a weekly or monthly basis. • Other franchisees will want to talk with you and share information.
How much money will satisfy your minimal lifestyle needs and how much do you hope to make? Can this business realistically deliver this income and is the return worth the investment?	• It is helpful to define how much money you need to meet your commitments as distinct from how much money you ideally want. • You need to consider the difference between cash flow, profit and capital gain and be clear on what is most important to you.
Are you happy to forgo your own way of doing things and follow someone else's systems?	• If you have a strong entrepreneurial or creative streak this could be a problem.
If things don't work out, are you prepared to take full responsibility for your decision to buy this business?	• All business involves some risk. • The statistical facts are that some businesses are going to fail, even in the best franchise systems, despite the best efforts of everyone.

- Be clear on how much money you wish to draw from the business to support your lifestyle. Check with the franchisor whether they believe this to be realistic.
- Be sure you have enough working capital to support you and the business should sales be slower than projected.
- Read as much relevant material on franchising as you can and buy a copy of a Franchisee Guide that contains useful checklists.
- Interview as many franchisees as possible about their experience and ask specific questions about the day to day obligations and commitments involved in running a business of this type.

After joining the franchise network:

- Be clear on the level and type of support your franchisor is obliged to provide under the franchise agreement.
- State your needs for additional support clearly and in writing, giving the rationale and the benefits to you and the business. However, be prepared to accept that the franchisor may not be in a position to deliver this.
- Build networks and friendships with other franchisees and attend as many franchise functions as possible.
- Remember that the franchisor's role is to make decisions that are in the best interests of the broader group. If you genuinely believe a decision is going to seriously damage your business raise this with the franchisor, giving your reasons and evidence. If possible suggest an alternative or a compromise that appears to still satisfy the need for national consistency while meeting your local needs.

Tips for franchisors

Follow a structured franchisee selection process. This should include:

- Checklists which assess all relevant information about the potential franchisee. We recommend the use of an 'attributes profile' which lists the things that significantly impact on the franchisee's ability to run a successful business.
- Representation statements which are signed to indicate the promises, claims and expectations of both parties.
- Valid selection techniques such as structured interviews, reference checks, on the job trials and behavioural profiling.

(For more information on franchisee suitability, attributes profiles and selection systems visit www.franchiserelationships.com).

Practice cautious optimism during the selection process. Point out both the up side and the down side of the business as well as the opportunities and risks. Ensure franchisees have a realistic picture of the hours and commitment required to operate the business.

Don't promise things that can't be delivered. Be careful not to commit other members of the franchisor team to deliver on a commitment before consulting them.

Don't assume franchisees will read your memos. Accept that a franchisee's mind will tend to be on attending to their day to day staffer customer issues. They do not tend to place a high priority on reading .memos and paper work from head office.

Beware of 'on the fly' decision making. Sound strategic planning and the obligations of both parties, as defined under the franchise agreement, should guide decisions on the allocation of resources. Also, consider how decisions on your franchise concept, products or suppliers might impact on franchisees. And remember when perception meets reality, reality inevitably comes out second best!

Develop a model for defining profitability. This should then be communicated to franchisees and used as the basis for benchmarking and profitability discussions. EBITO (Earnings Before Interest, Tax and Owners drawings) is a popular approach. (One group in the travel industry use EBITOH — Earnings Before Interest, Tax, Owners drawings and Holidays).

Provide information on corporate services and rebates. There are laws governing the declaration and transparency of transactions with regard to supplier rebates and marketing funds. You must obviously comply with these laws. It is also important that processes for charging fees or mark-ups for corporate services and supplies are transparent.

Don't embellish the facts. When presenting information on new initiatives provide as much specific information as possible. This is particularly important if the initiative is controversial. By providing good information people will be more likely to listen with an open mind.

Always remain clear on your formal obligations. Remember that your formal obligations are defined in the franchise agreement and that your role is to ensure your franchise system works well so that customers receive a high standard of service.

Be clear on the type of decision making you are using. Be careful not to give franchisees the impression that they will be having the final decision on an issue that you will actually be deciding on. (See Chapter 10)

Review the value of your services. Franchisees will at times question the value they are receiving from the relationship. There is no need to get defensive or take this questioning personally. Consider how your services are impacting on their profitability. Surveys can also be useful for measuring the value franchisees believe they are getting from specific services. (See Chapter 17)

Keep in touch with franchisees. Ensure franchisees are having adequate contact with others in the franchise system. As a general guide, franchisees should have some sort of contact or communication with others in the franchise network, at least once every 10 days.

In summary

In every situation in which we find ourselves, we respond according to our assumptions and the information available to us. This will usually be only part of the total picture. Because of their different roles, franchisees and franchisors also have different assumptions, different perceptions of what is required to meet their needs and different expectations of what is fair and reasonable. These differences need to be accepted, understood and managed.

Action Tips:

- Accept differences in perception as normal.
- Before proposing a solution check that other people share your beliefs or views on the facts of the situation.
- Review the specific questions and checklists contained in this chapter.
- Franchisors — when introducing new initiatives, keep in mind that the franchisee will have their own perspective on things.
- Franchisees — before resisting new initiatives, consider the rationale from the franchisor's perspective.

CHAPTER EIGHT
The Franchise E-Factor

There is a path on which I travelled as a franchisee and which almost every other franchisee I have ever met has also travelled. The places this path leads to are not physical, they are psychological in nature and include emotions such as hope, joy, disappointment, frustration and renewed confidence.

If you are beginning your journey into a new franchise business, chances are you will also travel along this path. And in so doing you will fall under the spell of what I have dubbed 'The Franchise E-Factor'.

The Franchise E-Factor is not a mental aberration or something to fear. It is simply a natural maturing of the relationship you have with your franchisor as you gain greater competence and confidence in running your franchise.

Six distinct stages

If you have a commitment to your business and are prepared to work through the ups and downs of life as a franchisee you will travel through six distinct stages. Some people move through these stages swiftly and more or less painlessly. For others the path is frustrating and full of interpersonal strain and resentment. Some people even get bogged down halfway through and decide that franchising is not for them.

If you are a franchisee you may find it useful to use this model as a way of making sense of the frustrations you may feel from time to time in your role as a business owner who wants independence yet can't quite have it. As you read through these six stages below it will become clear why this progression is called The Franchise E-Factor.

1. The Glee Stage

I am very happy with the relationship I have with my franchisor. They obviously care about my success and have delivered all they said. I am excited about my new business and full of hope for the future.

Initially franchisees are filled with glee. Along with their decision to buy a franchise comes the anticipation of whether things will work out and of course the hope of making lots of money.

During the opening stages of the business the franchisor will also be busy providing encouragement and support to their fresh and motivated franchisee. Like a wedding ceremony, the speeches at opening ceremonies of franchised outlets usually contain profound commitments such as:

"We will always be here for you";

"You are the reason for our existence"; or

"If you have any problems at all, just call and we will be there".

Positive emotions run high at this stage. There is a great sense of achievement for everyone as the numerous hurdles in establishing the business have now been cleared.

The Glee stage covers the lead up period to buying into the franchise and will usually stay with a franchisee for between 3 and 12 months, depending on their past business experience.

The franchisee's experience during the Glee stage

Nervousness. It is natural for there to be some anticipation and fear about whether the new business will work out as planned. The franchisee is also likely to be feeling quite vulnerable.

Excitement. The newness and novelty of the business may create a sense of euphoria. Franchisees may be running on adrenalin for a time as they face the inevitable challenges associated with starting in their new business.

Optimism. Businesses are always bought on the assumption of future success. In the absence of evidence to the contrary, it is natural for franchisees to feel a sense of optimism about the business's future.

Tips for franchisees — how to manage Glee

- Don't get disappointed if it takes a while for your customers to build up. In some territories or sites it will take 3 to 6 months of consistent effort until customers are ready to try out your business.

- On the other hand if you are very busy initially, due to a big opening promotion, be prepared for a natural drop off as your customer base sorts itself out. Some people will remain with you as loyal, long-term customers while others will just try you out once.

- Enjoy the initial buzz and excitement but accept that work will soon settle down into a routine. For some people this will be boring, while for others it will be a relief.

2. The Fee Stage

Although I'm making money, these royalty payments are really taking the cream off the top. What am I getting for my money ?

The second Fee stage kicks in as the franchisee gains more of a handle on the business's finances. It comes from a growing appreciation that profit is the result of sales minus expenses. At this point they may become particularly sensitive to the royalty and advertising fees, which they see as annoying expenses that eat into their profits.

Questions such as, "What am I getting for my money?" will surface in their mind, especially when they review their weekly royalty fees.

At this stage the franchisee's level of satisfaction starts to drop.

There are basically two paths from the Fee stage — either back to Glee (this can happen when the franchisor provides significant assistance with a problem that has been causing anguish), or into the Me stage.

The franchisee's experience during Fee

Questioning. Franchisees will tend to become more demanding about what they are receiving for their royalty fees. They will also question the value of the services they are receiving and may ask the franchisor to justify how the royalty fee has been calculated.

Commercially minded. As franchisees become more commercially astute they tend to think about how their royalty fees could be best used for the benefit of their business. They may start to put the heat on the franchisor for better quality and more comprehensive services; for instance they may suggest that the franchisor provides more training for their staffer they may complain about deficiencies in the personality and competence of field staff.

Skeptical. Any earlier feelings of delight a franchisee may have felt about their franchisor have usually cooled off by now. The relationship has moved from one of a grateful, starry eyed student who was eager to learn, to someone who is realising that their franchisor teacher is not as infallible as they thought.

Tips for franchisees — how to manage Fee

- Consider that there are many aspects of your franchise fees that are not so obvious, such as the years of investment into system development and brand building. This will often represent many millions of dollars. You are not just paying for someone to visit your store once a month.

- Use your franchisor's resources for the benefit of your business and don't be backward in requesting legitimate assistance. Franchisors may only respond to specific requests.

- Accept that your franchisor team are only human. Sure they may be able to improve in some areas but they are probably doing their best to help you. While you might think that complaining, undermining or criticising will improve their performance and service to you, it won't. You may get some short-term gains but the cost to you will be a strained relationship that may work against you in the future. People will always give you more of themselves if you treat them with respect. Rather than trying to win an argument or prove someone wrong (which just creates resentment), state your needs clearly, why you need this and what the franchisor might do differently to meet this need. A more positive approach pays off in the long run.

3. The Me Stage

Yes I am successful. But my success is a result of my hard work. I could probably be just as successful without my franchisor.

As the franchisee moves into the Me stage he or she will typically be thinking that their success is due purely to their own hard work and effort. This natural tendency to take the credit for the good things, is known in psychology as the 'Attribution Effect' or the 'Self-Serving Bias'. Attribution theory explains the thinking process we go through in searching for the best explanation of an event and also suggests that we are not all as rational as we might like to believe.

When we perform well or achieve something we tend to attribute this to our inherent skills and personality. We take the credit. But when we make mistakes or don't perform to expectation we tend to blame someone else or outside circumstances.

The human ego has always been a master at playing with our minds — giving us reasons why we are right and others are wrong, why we are good and others are bad, why we are smart and others are stupid, and so on. For some people it is a way of protecting their self-esteem.

However the Self-Serving Bias is not always a bad thing. For instance, people who are more optimistic tend to achieve more and live longer, happier lives. Their trick is to interpret bad events as being temporary, very specific and due to outside circumstances. On the other hand they interpret the good things that happen to them as having general lasting benefit and as being in some way linked to their own good qualities. It's actually not a bad recipe for staying positive, especially if you are in sales.

Not surprisingly, we find the Self-Serving Bias alive and well in the franchise relationship. It tends to be at its strongest when the franchisee moves through the Me stage where they will tend to attribute their success to their own work and initiative. If things are not going so well however, the franchisor is inevitably held to blame. Either way the franchisor usually starts to receive some criticism.

The Self-Serving Bias is brilliantly portrayed in the film *The Life of Brian* in which a secret meeting takes place by a group who want to bring down the Roman Empire. As the leader of the group (John Cleese) tries to discredit the Romans with his cries of "What have they ever done for us?!!", a comical dialogue emerges as the following answers emerge from his sheepish followers ... "Education" ... "Law and Order" ... "Roads" ... "The Aqueducts", and the list goes on. Yet John Cleese still manages to convince them that they must somehow have been given a raw deal.

The franchisee's experience during Me

Self centred. They will typically attribute their success to their own hard work and initiative and fail to acknowledge the franchisor's contribution. They may also become more demanding in their expectations.

Proud. Franchisees that step back and review the progress they have made through their hard work will naturally experience a heightened sense of pride and confidence. They may feel they know more than their franchisor and thus no longer need to listen to their advice, although they will certainly be ready to give their own.

Frustrated. Franchisees may feel they could make even more progress if their franchisor was more willing to listen to their views and provide a better standard of support. The sense that they are catching up to or passing their franchisor in their operational knowledge can lead to feelings of disappointment. The franchisor is now well and truly slipping off the pedestal.

Tips for franchisees — how to manage Me

- Be proud of your achievements but also give credit where credit's due. As I said in my introduction to this book, all human achievements are built on the shoulders of others.

- Don't rest on your laurels. Your achievements will be worthless to you if not sustained through vigilance and hard work. Changes in your local market can quickly turn you from a market leader into 'yesterday's hero'. For instance, the bakery I once ran so successfully is now out of business because of changes in local shopping habits.

- Focus your efforts on how you can refine your success. The successful Japanese philosophy of continuous improvement called Kaizan, meaning 'a tiny step forward', promotes the idea that the best improvements come from a hundred 'one percents' -- not one big hit.

- By all means share your ideas and experiences but accept that others may not always be ready or open to hearing them at the time. However if what you are doing is producing terrific results, your franchisor will soon come to you to find out more about it. So be patient and be consistent.

4. The Free Stage

I really don't like all the restrictions my franchisor is putting on the way I run my business. I feel frustrated and annoyed at their constant interference. I want to be able to do my own thing and express my own ideas.

While the franchise relationship tends to begin with the franchisee relatively dependent on the franchisor this does not last. As a franchisee's business confidence grows, their drive towards independence will increasingly assert itself. A franchisee at this stage might feel resentful having to follow the franchisor's standard operating procedures all the time.

The Free stage is characterised by a need to break free of the restrictions and limitations of the franchise and a testing of the system's boundaries. The franchisee might for instance test out how tight the franchise agreement is and try to break free of their contractual obligations.

The franchisor might also decide to break free of the franchisee, either through a forced sale or termination of the agreement. Obviously chances of conflict are greatest at this point.

A franchisee who is stuck in this stage can become trouble to him or herself and a negative influence on others. They may also be a ripe target to be exploited by someone wanting to provoke trouble in the franchise network. As we saw in Chapter 6, unscrupulous lawyers or consultants have been known to use franchisees who are unhappy about specific issues as their ticket to make some money.

At this stage the franchisee will either get bogged down in resentment and continue to bicker with their franchisor, revert to the Me stage with intermittent but harmless grumbling, or move to the next stage — the quantum leap — the See stage.

The franchisee's experience during the Free stage

Cynical. Franchisees may question the motives of their franchisor and challenge the reasons behind new innovations or changes in strategy. An 'us and them' mentality will tend to colour most interactions.

Constrained. The franchisee can develop a prisoner mentality, feeling that their franchisor is inhibiting their creativity. For instance they may have developed what they believe is an innovative addition to the franchise concept, only to have their field manager tell them to stop this practice immediately.

Combative. Franchisees will want to check where the boundaries of the system lie. They want to know how far they can stretch their sense of independence as their confidence in their business grows. They often feel the need to test the franchisor's commitment to them. Discussions and interactions are likely to be tense and peppered with conflict.

Tips for franchisees — how to manage Free

- Remember that you have made a long-term commitment in signing a franchise agreement and no one forced you. There are many tangible and intangible benefits to be gained if you are prepared to make the most of this long-term relationship.

- Never allow specific problems to remain unresolved and fester. Open and honest communication is vital. You may sometimes have to take the initiative. If you don't think you will get anywhere by yourself get a supportive but objective third party involved in the discussion.

- If you have not been able to resolve a burning issue despite your best efforts, seek the involvement of a professional mediator. Do not threaten or seek legal advice unless you have exhausted all other options.

5. The See Stage

I guess I can see the importance of following the franchise system.
And I do acknowledge the value of my franchisor's support services.
I can see that if we all did our own thing standards would drop and we would lose the very things that give us our competitive edge.

Conflict in relationships seldom goes away by ignoring it. For the franchisee to move to the See stage there needs to be some frank and open discussion, where franchisee and franchisor listen carefully to each other's point of view. There may be some blood letting as previous disputes or disagreements are reopened. Mistakes and misunderstanding will no doubt have occurred on both sides of the relationship. There needs to be an acceptance and letting go of the past by both parties.

The franchisor might need to be more open in involving the franchisee in future planning or appreciating their specific needs. If the franchise system has been managed fairly and effectively the franchisee will generally come around to seeing that without consistency and adherence to the systems, the strength of the entire group would be lost. It is this shift in perception that characterises the See stage.

The franchisee's experience during the See stage

Inquisitive. When a franchisee recognises the futility of constantly bickering with their franchisor they will tend to seek out alternative more positive methods of communicating. It is at this point that a more open dialogue can take place.

Open minded. As the franchisee appreciates that they are part of a larger system where everyone's individual needs cannot necessarily be met, they will tend to be more open minded to the franchisor's thinking.

Empathy. If a franchisor shows they are willing to put the time and energy into genuinely listening to a franchisee's concerns, the franchisee will generally respond with a greater willingness to listen to and appreciate the franchisor's point of view.

Tips for franchisees — how to manage See

- Make an effort to really understand your franchisor's reasons for doing the things they do. Listen to the facts and keep an open mind.

- If your chain has a Franchise Advisory Council take the opportunity to sit on this or at least communicate concerns or ideas to your representative.

- If you have an unresolved issue, come back to your franchisor with an alternative proposal or suggested solution. Be specific and give reasons why it could work. Minimise the risks to the franchisor and consider the impact of your idea on the rest of the system. Perhaps suggest a way to trial your idea with a review date and criteria to assess the success of the trial. You may be surprised at how readily positive solutions are listened to.

6. The We Stage

We need to work together to make the most of our business relationship. I need some specific assistance in certain areas to develop my business but I also have some ideas that I want my franchisor to consider.

From the See stage there is a natural progression to the We stage — a move from independent to interdependent thinking. At this point the franchisee is prepared to put his or her ego aside and recognises that success and satisfaction generally come more easily from working with, rather than against, their franchisor.

To reach the We stage a franchisee must be mature, objective and commercially minded. Most importantly, they must be profitable. As long as a franchisee is not making acceptable profits and feels their franchisor is not responding to their needs they will shake the system for change.

A franchisor that wants their franchisees to move into the We stage must deliver on their obligations and be fair and consistent in their dealings.

Franchisees who have negotiated their way through the franchise relationship minefield to the We stage are a franchise network's greatest asset. They will often be quiet achievers who keep one eye on their profit and one eye on cultivating healthy business relationships, not just with their franchisor but with their suppliers, peers and of course, their customers.

The franchisee's experience during the We stage

Cooperative. The franchisee will see the mutual benefits in working with their franchisor. Ideas and opinions will be openly shared in a spirit of mutual trust and cooperation.

Assertive. While the franchisee will be prepared to cooperate, they will also not be backward in stating their needs and views in a frank and direct manner. If they do not think an idea is in their or the network's best interests they will state this. However concerns will tend to be driven by sensible strategic and commercial considerations rather than short term self interest, pride or ego.

Forward thinking. Franchisees at the We stage have usually thought through their long term business and lifestyle goals. They will tend to have a game plan that extends for at least two years and will be working ON as well as IN their business.

Tips for franchisees — how to manage We

- Be an active participant in networking with others in your system. Our research shows that the most successful franchisees are those that share their experiences and insights with their peers and their franchisor. Any teacher, trainer or consultant will tell you that when they share their experience with others they find it also helps them to develop their own ideas further.

- Sit on committees and assist with mentoring new franchisees. It will help to keep you vibrant, positive and growing. No one 'arrives' in business — or indeed in life. So treat your role in the business as a continual journey of discovery and self-improvement.

- Cultivate a positive relationship with your franchisor and use it wisely to benefit your business. Your franchisor company needs you as much as you need it.

From dependence to independence

In the diagram of The Franchise E-Factor note the progression from dependence through independence to interdependence and how satisfaction is at its lowest when the drive for independence is at its highest.

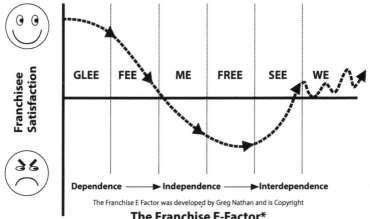

The Franchise E-Factor*

The Franchise E-Factor is in fact based on the natural progression which many relationships move through — from dependence to independence to interdependence. If you have teenage children you may recognise some parallels here.

Dependence — Early in the franchise relationship the franchisee is typically dependent on the franchisor for guidance and support. They may even place the franchisor on a pedestal believing that the franchisor's technical knowledge will surely guarantee them success.

Independence — As the franchisee gains more experience in running their business, the desire for independence will inevitably start to assert itself. The ultimate test of the franchise relationship is how successfully both parties are in navigating the journey through this independence illusion.

Interdependence — Interdependence is the highest and most mature type of relationship. Franchisors and franchisees that are able to develop a healthy interdependent relationship are fortunate, for their businesses will continue to grow and prosper. But this type of relationship requires maturity, honesty and commitment. The ideal of a healthy interdependent relationship is something franchisors and franchisees should strive for.

*For permission to use the Franchise E-Factor in publications, talks or training, refer to www.franchiserelationships.com

In summary

The Franchise E-Factor represents the natural maturing of the franchise relationship as franchisees gain greater confidence and competence in running their business. It also helps both parties to make sense of the strains that will inevitably occur as the relationship moves from dependent to truly interdependent.

Action Tips:

Note: Because specific action tips are provided for franchisees throughout this chapter, these tips apply to franchisors.

- During *Glee* keep a cool head, be cautious with your promises and don't get carried away with the ups and downs of a start up business.
- During *Fee* keep focused on your formal obligations and don't make knee jerk decisions for franchisees who want to see more short-term value for their royalties.
- During *Me* expect no gratitude for your efforts. Focus on coaching franchisees to continue to improve their performance.
- During *Free* remain calm and do not become defensive. Maintain open communications and a firm but fair dialogue. If necessary suggest that a mediator be used to assist with communication.
- During *See* listen carefully to the franchisee's concerns and be open to their ideas while not compromising any of the franchise system's fundamental policies.
- During *We* consult with franchisees on important decisions and encourage their involvement with committees and in mentoring new franchisees.

More About the Franchise E-Factor

In response to reader feedback about the Franchise E-Factor, I have developed the following two products:

- A book for franchise executives, called *The Franchise E-Factor*, that describes in more depth the six stages and how they should be managed within a franchise system. (See final page for details.)

- A *Franchise E-Factor Licence and Training Kit* for use in the induction of franchisees and the ongoing training of franchisor staff. (See www.franchiserelationships.com for details.)

CHAPTER NINE

More Communication and Less Conflict

Good communication is important for success in all areas of life and particularly in the close interdependent franchise relationship. However the truth is that most of us are pathetically inconsistent in our performance. Ironically it is when we feel most strongly about something that we seem to communicate most poorly. In particular feelings such as impatience, frustration, intolerance or resentment tend to create barriers to good communication.

In this chapter we are going to address the skills of empathy, listening and assertiveness and how these can help overcome the barriers to good communication. These skills also hold the key to managing the various conflict situations that franchisors and franchisees inevitably face, including the stages of The Franchise E Factor.

Frank's words of wisdom

Someone who has certainly earned the right to make knowledge-able statements about franchise relationships is Frank Rechichi, ex-managing director of Cut Price Deli. Frank spent decades building a large and impressive retail franchising empire. Yet it all crumbled as a result of a run of bad press and a series of legal battles with some unhappy franchisees.

In reflecting on what he had learned from his experience, Frank recounted a significant incident in which one of his franchise support managers had criticised a franchisee over the state of the franchisee's store. While the franchisor staff member thought it an innocent enough comment at the time, the franchisee took par-ticular offence because he thought the criticism was insensitive and unwarranted. Frank believes this incident was the trigger for a three year legal action by the franchisee that eventually had devastating consequences for all parties, both commercially and personally.

Frank's advice is this.

"Be very careful if you are going to say something that could damage the pride or ego of another person.

"Franchisees put themselves on the line, financially and emotionally, and you can mortally wound someone with an insensitive comment.

"What you may think is the right way to do something may not make sense from their point of view, so you need to take the time to really listen to them and not fall into the trap of becoming self-righteous or bombastic."

It doesn't pay to give advice

No doubt you often find yourself in a position where you need to tell someone that you disagree with them or give them feedback on something you believe they have done wrong. For instance, as a field manager you might need to bring to a franchisee's attention certain things that are interfering with the performance of their business. Or as a franchisee you might want to explain how disappointed you have been with the marketing support you have been receiving from your franchisor.

Although the first reaction for many of us is to rush in and give advice or tell people what they must do, this is often not the best way of handling the situation.

In this book I have emphasised the point that trying to force people to do things doesn't work. In the final analysis you cannot force people to do things they don't want to do. Arguing never really works because in the long run you lose any chance of future cooperation from the person you 'won' the argument with. This is because he or she will feel that you didn't take their concerns or objections seriously.

'Yes butting'

When someone raises an objection to accepting our point of view we usually react in one of two ways. We either try to convince them that they should adopt our idea, or we try to force them to adopt our idea by confronting them. These approaches tend not to work because they force the other person to dig their heels in and defend their own position. By trying to prove that we are right we are in fact making the other person wrong. And who likes to be told they are wrong?

The result is 'Yes butting' conversations, which go something like this:

"We want to introduce a new range of uniforms into the network".

"Ah **yes, but** all our staff are happy with the old uniform".

"**Yes,** I appreciate this, **but** it's time we updated our image".

"**Yes, but** it took two years to get this uniform right and it is crazy to change it now".

"**Yes, but** our competitors have just modernised their image and we have to keep up".

"Well I think it's a stupid idea!"

Arguments like this simply go nowhere.

Active listening

Instead of reacting and getting a person's back up, there is an approach called Active Listening, which shows the other person that you respect them and take them seriously. They will then be far less defensive and more open to listening to your point of view.

Active listening involves listening carefully to what the other person is saying, without interrupting, reacting or giving advice. Your aim is to find out what their underlying concern or problem is. Often we need to go beyond the superficial to find out what is really bugging someone.

When you think about it giving uninvited advice is a put down. The underlying message you are giving to the other person is, "You are a dill and can't run your own affairs so I am going to tell you what you should do."

Active listening is a powerful tool used by psychologists and counsellors for helping people sort out problems or difficulties, and although it seems simple and easy, it requires concentration and self-control. It means we have to censor our tendencies to make comments or pass judgement on the other person's point of view.

Allowing a person to freely express their concerns is often all that is needed to release the pressure they feel and enable them to think clearly and find their own solutions. However to listen actively you need to have empathy for the other person's position.

Empathy blockers

In normal conversation we don't usually go very deeply into understanding how other people are feeling. In fact often our advice, reactions, comments and reassurance, although well intentioned, actually prevent people from feeling understood. Instead of helping to sort out the problem they raise barriers. You could call them 'Empathy Blockers'.

Some examples of Empathy Blockers are:

Preaching— "You should be spending more time ... blah, blah"
Moralising — "It's just not right the way you ... blah, blah, blah"
Criticising — "You are just not up to scratch ... blah, blah, blah"
Diagnosing — "The trouble with you is that... blah, blah, blah"
Advising — "If I were you I would ... blah, blah, blah"

Although you may mean well with these habitual responses they can actually be barriers to good communication because they do not allow the other person to express what they really feel. Note that these statements are also mostly 'you' statements which carry an undertone of blame and judgement.

How to be an active listener

- Give your complete attention to what the other person is saying. Show them you are genuinely interested in what they have to say. Focus on how they appear to be feeling as well as what they are saying.

- Be silent as much as possible and let them talk. Expressions such as "Really", "I see", or "Tell me more" are useful to let them know you are listening.

- Encourage them to speak, especially if they seem reluctant or upset. You can do this with comments such as "I'd like to hear what you have to say" or "I'm interested, please tell me about it".

- Maintain an open, friendly approach. Nod, gently smile and be encouraging in your approach.

- Let the person know you understand what they are saying and how they are feeling by paraphrasing their comments or clarifying important points. For instance: "So what you are saying is ..." or "It seems to me that you are unhappy about..." or "You sound pretty concerned by..."

- If the person does not indicate that they feel understood, ask them if they could explain their point of view again.

- If emotions are running high, speak calmly and maintain eye contact. Let them talk until they have said what they want to say. If you need further information ask for it calmly.

Active listening provides the other person with the freedom and the opportunity to clarify their problem. This, in turn, can release the pressure they feel inside which can greatly help in resolving the issue at hand.

Once you have actively listened to the other person's point of view or situation you will then be in a stronger position to put across your point of view if necessary. This involves the skill of assertiveness.

The difference between assertive and aggressive

Conflict inevitably occurs whenever differences or disagreements provoke ill feeling. Typically there are two responses to such a situation — we withdraw in a submissive way or we attack in an aggressive way. In other words we follow our basic fight/flight genetic programming. While this programming might work well in the jungle where one has to survive on one's wits to eat (or be eaten), it does not work in a civilised society. Human history of wars, bloodshed and misery testify to this. Some philosophers call this 'The Human Condition'.

There is however a third alternative to dealing with differences which gets results while respecting the rights and needs of oneself and others. It is commonly referred to as being assertive.

In other words we have a choice when faced with a situation involving a disagreement; we can be submissive, aggressive or assertive.

The submissive approach

When a person takes a submissive approach they typically bottle things up with little regard for their own feelings. They let others walk over them in the name of politeness. There are some short term benefits of being submissive. For instance, it postpones feelings of anxiety and it keeps the peace. However such an approach tends to reinforce poor self esteem and, of course, you often end up getting the raw end of the bargain.

The aggressive approach

Taking an aggressive stance typically involves blurting things out or disregarding the interests or feelings of the other person. Aggressive behaviour such as blaming, accusing or yelling might bring short-term benefits such as instant gratification or action; however there are costs. It stimulates unhealthy emotions such as fear, anger and guilt and it undermines your future relationship with the other person.

The assertive approach

Being assertive is not easy. It takes courage and often lots of practice because it goes against habits we may have picked up from parents or other role models from our past. Being assertive involves expressing your thoughts and feelings clearly and openly while also listening to the other person and respecting their needs. The great benefit of practicing assertive behaviour is that it builds your self-esteem, it preserves your relationships with others and, most importantly, it gets sustainable results.

In summary, moving away from our fight (aggressive)/flight (submissive) programming may produce some initial anxiety as it requires us to face up to issues without sweeping them under the carpet. It also requires courage, patience and tolerance.

How to be more assertive

There are three simple steps to taking more of an assertive approach.

Step 1. Listen to others and show them you respect their thoughts and feelings. Use your active listening skills.

Step 2. Consider everyone's rights including your own, and try to make an assessment of what appears to be important to the people involved. It may be that you need to take time out to think things over before deciding on the approach you intend to take.

Step 3. Express your point of view in an open, honest and non-defensive way. Focus on how you feel or how the situation affects you rather than blaming the other person. Using 'I' sentences rather than 'you' sentences can be useful. For example an aggressive response would be:

"You don't have a good reason for disagreeing with us on this, you're just being a smart arse as usual. Get your act together!"

On the other hand an assertive response would be:

"I have difficulty understanding why you disagree with us on this Paul. I would find it helpful if you could explain your position again."

When you combine an assertive approach with active listening you have a very persuasive combination which creates a positive atmosphere of mutual respect and understanding. In this atmosphere you can work towards joint solutions with each person knowing that their concerns are not being ignored. There is no longer the feeling that you each have to keep defending your separate interests.

Focus on interest not positions

A useful approach to dealing with conflict is called 'Principled Negotiation'. The appeal of this approach is its emphasis on being fair with others while ensuring that they do not take advantage of your fairness. One of its most powerful recommendations is that the parties in a dispute focus on their interests rather than on taking positions or making judgements on who is right and wrong.

The two sisters and the orange

A popular story in the conflict literature is about two sisters who were quarrelling over an orange. It explains the value of focussing on interests. After hours of quarrelling the sisters decided on a compromise and agreed to divide the orange in half. One sister cut the orange, and the other sister had first choice of the halves. (This kept the first sister honest when she divided the orange.)

After the orange had been divided, the first sister took her half, ate the fruit and threw away the peel. The second sister threw away the fruit and used the peel from her half to bake a cake. If they had focussed on their interests and not their positions, one sister could have had the whole orange to eat and the other sister could have had all the peel and baked, not just one, but two cakes! Instead they rather stupidly took the rigid position of "I want this orange."

It is very easy in a conflict situation to assume that, because the other side has a different position to you, their interests are also different and must be opposed. Yet, by asking questions and listening carefully you may discover that behind their position they have interests that are either similar or complementary to your own.

So next time you find yourself in conflict with someone rather than take a position, give them the opportunity to voice their concerns and use your listening skills to draw them out about their interests. And if they keep talking about their position, you can respond positively by talking about your interests. I guarantee that you will make far more progress with far less stress.

Keeping an open mind

In coming to an agreement on any issue it is important to try to handle ideas creatively and to keep an open mind. Sometimes we feel threatened or react to another person for any number of reasons. In the franchise context franchisees might not listen to their franchisor because they feel a new idea could undermine their security. On the other hand franchisors might not listen to a franchisee because they feel their suggestion undermines the integrity of the franchise system.

As we have learned, prematurely ridiculing or dismissing anyone's ideas is a sure way to put them on the defensive. Franchisors would do well to remember that many innovative products and services on the market today have been suggested by franchisees who were given the opportunity to express their thoughts and ideas on how aspects of the franchise system could be improved.

Warning signs of impending conflict

Conflict seldom comes out of the blue — there are always signs of an impending problem. If you find that people in your franchise system are behaving in one or more of the following ways you can be almost certain there is underlying conflict that needs to be addressed. Ignore these warning signs at your peril.

Majoring in minors

Minor problems will be projected as major catastrophes. People focus on problem finding rather than problem solving, and behaviour is motivated by a desire to punish others or seek revenge for being badly done by.

Communication breakdowns

There may be a reluctance to respond openly to clear and simple questions. For instance, messages may not be returned and communication may have come to a standstill. Perhaps people no longer listen to each other, taking up a position in which they believe they are right and others are definitely wrong.

Scape goating

There might be 'scape goating' or unfairly blaming individuals for broader problems. In such cases a mob mentality may occur and people tend to band together in groups with the aim of having someone moved out of the system.

Waning commitment

People may question the value of the franchise relationship and put down the benefits of being involved in the system. There might be a waning of commitment to support or attend activities or programs.

Mistrust

There may be certain issues or problems which recur as patterns of behaviour or regular complaints. Perhaps trust has become an issue when people doubt the intentions behind apparent acts of goodwill or assistance.

Internal squabbling

There could be a growing preoccupation with internal relationship issues which start to take precedence over focussing on the needs of the customer and the business. People may become so busy with their internal squabbling that they forget why they are in business.

If franchisees or franchisor staff members are showing any of the above signs you have a responsibility to take positive action. If the problems cannot be resolved they should be put in writing to the franchisor or franchisee and arrangements made to have a mediator appointed. The earlier a mediator is called in the better the chances of a satisfactory resolution.

Pretending that conflict does not exist or will go away if you ignore it is a foolish approach.

The process of mediation

Most franchising industry or government franchising codes around the world contain dispute resolution clauses. These typically require franchisors and franchisees that have ongoing unresolved problems to seek formal mediation. Many franchise agreements today also have a dispute resolution clause in them to reflect this.

The role of a mediator is not to make a decision like a judge but to assist the parties to come to an agreement. With a solution-focussed approach resolutions can almost always be reached, providing the parties wish to have things resolved. Statistics from thousands of mediations monitored by the Australian Office of the Franchising Mediation Adviser, suggest 75% of franchise mediations reach agreement after just one session.

The key elements of a sound mediation process would typically include the following.

Mediation agreement

The parties are required to sign a mediation agreement that lays down some ground rules and protects them and the mediator from the inappropriate use of information.

Confidentiality

Issues discussed during the mediation session cannot be discussed with other parties or used at a later date. If the mediator talks individually with the parties, this information also stays confidential unless this party decides otherwise. The mediator will often be used to pass information between the parties at their request.

Without prejudice

The parties can put offers forward and be frank with each other without any worry that the information can be used later against them, for example in court.

Authority to settle

To prevent the dragging on of negotiations the people attending the mediation should have the authority to negotiate and settle on an agreement.

Mediator's role

The mediator is not a judge, arbitrator, legal adviser, accountant or consultant. He or she should have no vested interest or bias in the dispute or any solution that might be arrived at. The mediator's role is to assist the parties to re-evaluate their situation and help them negotiate an agreement.

Lawyers

The parties can have their lawyers present if they choose to and should be able to consult with them as much as they like. However there should be no point scoring by the lawyers about who is right or wrong. The focus should always be on moving the parties to a resolution that they can all live with.

Voluntary participation

The parties can leave the mediation at any time, as can the mediator if he or she feels they are abusing the process.

A wise solution

The mediator will often counsel the parties to the effect that if they are rigidly locked into getting their own way the process may not work and that they should aim to reach a wise agreement — one that they can live with even though it may not be exactly what they want. A wise solution is also one that is realistic, one that satisfies their concerns and interests, and one that is fair to all involved.

Emotional content

Disputes often lead to intense emotions. Perceptions of what is fair or reasonable behaviour may be different or expectations may not have been met, leading to feelings of anger, resentment or even revenge. These feelings tend to inflame the situation so people in a mediation are asked to control their emotions by keeping to the following simple ground rules:

- One person speaks at a time.
- Where necessary the mediator has the power to direct the flow of communication.
- No abusive language or put-downs.
- Treat each other with respect and listen to each other's views.

The role of the Franchise Agreement

The Franchise Agreement is the basis of the franchise contract, giving the franchisor the formal power to maintain the standards and integrity of the concept, and bring into line any deviations which may ultimately reflect badly on the group. It is however a mistake to think that all a franchisor's power comes from this legal document.

Strong franchise systems are built from profitable franchise units and happy franchisees. Regularly resorting to the Franchise Agreement to control misdemeanours is not recommended. In reality the most powerful tool a franchisor has is a good relationship with its franchisees.

The Agreement should never be used lightly — only as a last resort and then with full force. In other words franchisors shouldn't make threats unless they actually mean to carry them out.

Warning — Don't put your emotions in writing

If you are a franchisee reading this, it is possible that from time to time your franchisor will make a bad call on an important issue and you will feel the need to 'let them have it'. Or if you are a franchisor, you will find that franchisees will sometimes step out of line on important issues and you will feel that a strong reprimand is in order.

In either case, if this is done in writing, you should word it very carefully. Harsh written criticism will nearly always be taken in the worst possible context.

Never send anything in writing while you are feeling emotional. After putting down your thoughts, set them aside for at least a day. Then consider showing this to someone who is objective about the issue. It may be that a discussion is a far more effective way to get your point across and produce a change in behaviour.

If you do decide to put your views in writing, soften it with some specific positive comments and invite the person to call if they have any questions. Then follow them up with a phone call. (If you don't you are likely to get an equally aggressive response defending their position and attacking you.)

Finally include a statement about how much better things will be when the problem is resolved and finish the letter on a positive note, perhaps reaffirming your faith in them.

It is seldom, if ever, productive to arouse resentment through critical written communications that are likely to be used against you or your company in the future.

Remember that where someone has received something in writing they can read it, and re-read it, and re-read it, dwelling on the words and the perceived sentiments with no opportunity to express their point of view on the situation. Like a volcano the pressure builds up and this person will either erupt at you sometime in the future when you least expect it, or get to work behind the scenes venting their anger to anyone who will listen.

The email trap

The above principles apply doubly to email. Because email messages are so quick and easy to bang out they are often poorly worded and have little thought put into them. This makes them even more vulnerable to misinterpretation.

While email is a useful way to transfer data, it is no replacement for communication. Human communication involves a full exchange of information — tone and speed of voice, facial expressions and body language. If you have tried to communicate a subtle or emotional message through email you will no doubt have found that it often fails. Even Bill Gates advises that "Email is not a good way to get mad at someone since you can't interact."

Communities are built on trust

A recurring theme in this book is that a major underlying skill in resolving conflict is having the ability to understand and appreciate the needs and expectations of the other party.

Another important principle in maintaining good relationships is to establish trust. This is a challenge because there can be suspicion from franchisees and franchisors about the motives of each other, especially when problems emerge. Because trust is so fundamental and lies at the foundation of all positive relationships, you should seek to create a culture of trust in your franchise system. The following acronym spells out some practical approaches on how we can all build greater trust in our relationships with others.

Truthfulness — be up front and honest in what you say and do. Trust dies almost instantly when people find that you have not been straight with them.

Respect — show respect in your dealings with others, even when their views and approaches differ from your own. If you put others down you will breed resentment and defensiveness.

Understanding — take the time to actively listen to what people are really saying so you understand their feelings and needs.

Service — try to be of genuine help and support to others, rather than exploiting every situation for your own short term gain. When you invest in the welfare of others you are also investing in your relationship with that person.

Tact — take into account differences in personality styles when communicating with others. The Platinum Rule, a variation on the

Golden Rule, is a useful way to improve communication. It states "Do unto others as they would have done unto them!" This means you may need to modify your approach depending on who you're talking to.

In summary

While good communication is essential for success in all areas of life, it takes relentless practice and commitment to be a good communicator. More specifically we need to master the skills of listening, empathy and assertiveness.

Action Tips:

- Resist the temptation to offer advice unless specifically asked, or the other person gives you permission.

- Before giving your opinion, clarify with the person that you do really understand their situation.

- If you find yourself in a 'Yes Butting' conversation, withdraw gracefully by saying something like "You know, you could be right. Could you tell me why you think that?"

- Practise your active listening skills at every opportunity. Home is a great place to start.

- If a person is very emotional speak calmly, maintain eye contact and encourage them to talk about their needs or interests. For instance ask, "What would make this better for you?"

- Be sensitive to the symptoms of unresolved conflict and have the courage to tackle it in a thoughtful and respectful way. If necessary instigate a formal mediation process.

- Explore interests rather than defend positions and keep an open mind on any option that could satisfy the other person's interests.

- When you are feeling emotional about something be very careful what you say and in particular what you put in writing.

- Before sending emotionally charged written material, let it sit for a few hours or seek someone else's opinion.

- Do not use email to try to resolve a conflict.

- Practise the Platinum Rule when dealing with people who have a different personality style to you.

CHAPTER TEN

The Challenge of Decision Making

Life is a process of taking in information, making decisions and acting on these decisions. While we are each individually responsible for the decisions we make about our own lives, many of our decisions will impact on the lives of others.

I believe that when others are affected by our decisions we have a responsibility to consider what the impact may be on them. This of course is particularly relevant to the interdependent franchising environment.

Power shifts from the past to the present

In prior generations it was common for people in authority to make decisions about what they thought was in the best interests of those for whom they were responsible. However this process of 'authoritarian' decision making has been steadily declining over the years. In its place have come more democratic methods where those affected by a decision have the opportunity to have some influence over its outcome. As a result, many groups in our society, who in the past had little power or influence, today have an increasing role in the decision making process. Here are a few examples of what I mean.

- Environmental groups now have a significant influence over the policies of governments and companies.

- Consumers have more power and influence than ever before over the behaviour of manufacturers and retailers.

- Employees in factories are empowered to make significant production decisions without consulting management; for example stopping a production line if they see the need.

- Children and students today also have far more control over how their parents and teachers interact with them — some might say too much!

As these shifts continue to touch our social and business relationships, questions are raised about who has the power to do what to whom. These shifts are also influencing the thinking of our legal institutions.

In the franchising context, franchisors and franchisees are thus operating in an increasingly complex social and legal environment. New precedents for unfair or unconscionable conduct for instance have created uncertainty regarding the rights of franchisors and franchisees, with franchisors now being unsure of whether they really do have the power to make important unilateral decisions in the way their franchise system operates.

Life is not so simple

The basic question is this: "Should one group of people have the right to make decisions that will impact on other people without these others having a say in the decision making process?"

It would be tempting to provide a simplistic answer to this question. For instance to say that everyone should have a say in the things that affect them. However, life is not so simple.

Most people would agree that it would be irresponsible and even dangerous to allow children to make decisions on issues when they do not yet have the maturity or knowledge to grasp the consequences of their actions. And it would be a poor management decision to 'empower' staff to make decisions on issues affecting an organisation's future if these staff did not have the competence or objectivity to discriminate on the best course of action.

Should franchisees have more say?

The question of who should be making what decisions is a hot one for franchise networks. As franchisees move through the stages in the Franchise E-Factor they will generally find themselves wanting more say in how their network functions, particularly in the operational areas where they will have become quite proficient.

When decisions are to be taken which are going to impact on a franchise network, it makes sense for franchisees to be involved. After all, franchisees typically have a high emotional and financial interest in their business and will no doubt have strong views to express.

While franchisee involvement is an important and positive force in franchising it needs to be applied intelligently. There are of course a number of sayings such as "Too many cooks spoil the broth" that caution us on the pitfalls of trying to give everyone a say.

The rest of this chapter will look at some of the issues that franchisors and franchisees should consider in relation to decision-making processes.

Preventing strategic disintegration

The key to good strategic decision making is objectivity regarding the interests of all parties, good information and a long-term perspective.

In earlier chapters it was emphasised that a franchisor's major responsibility is to protect the long-term strategic interests of the entire network, particularly the brand. This requires the franchisor to be constantly researching and scouring the international market place for changing trends, opportunities and threats that are likely to impact on the network.

The franchisor must particularly be clear on the following three areas:

The group's brand reputation. What is it that we want people to think and feel when they come into contact with our brand?

The group's unique competitive advantage. What do we do differently or better than our competitors that enables us to deliver a better value proposition to our customers?

The group's core business. What essentially are we in the business of doing, ie. what customer needs do we fundamentally satisfy?

This strategic focus is critical to a franchise network's long-term survival. A franchisor that fails to act when there is confusion or fragmentation in any one of these areas is on a sure path to disintegration.

Operational strategists

There are good reasons why these areas need to remain the domain of the franchisor. In the hurly burly of daily trading franchisees face a hundred and one challenges impacting on their sales, customer satisfaction and staff morale. A local competitor may be price cutting, customers may be asking for specific products that are not part of the core range or staff may not like their new uniforms.

These local operational challenges inevitably colour a franchisee's opinions and views about what the network should be doing.

They also make it difficult for a franchisee to sustain a strategic perspective that takes into account the long-term interests of the entire network.

The point is this. While franchisees are in a good position to be excellent 'operational strategists', when working close to the coalface of a business it can be difficult to be objective and extract oneself from short term operational concerns.

Franchisees may also be surprised to hear the diversity of opinions that a franchisor must deal with in the course of a typical week over issues such as uniforms, suppliers, advertising and the performance of its own field staff. It is not uncommon for seventy franchisees to produce fifty opinions on the same issue. This of course makes it impossible to keep everyone happy.

Attributes that add value

Given the social trends towards participative decision making, there is sure to be a shift in many franchise companies to allow franchisees more strategic input into the business, despite the difficulties described above. My advice here is to ensure that the people chosen are carefully screened for their ability to display the following attributes during important discussions:

- **Maturity** — can keep a cool head and doesn't revert to emotional tantrums.

- **Objectivity** — can put aside one's own self-interest or prejudices.

- **Relevant experience** — has significant operational or senior executive experience.

- **Calibre of thinking** — can understand complex issues and is able to think broadly and laterally.

- **Integrity** — is up front and honest regarding their motives.

These qualities add value to the strategic process. However care needs to be taken not to have 'too many chiefs' when important decisions are being made.

The two elements of a good decision

In a fast paced business environment significant decisions need to be made daily. Many of these will impact on franchisees such as whether a supplier should be changed, how media dollars should be allocated or what changes should be made to the computer system.

A good decision has two parts to it.

Firstly, it needs to be sound in terms of its capacity to meet specified objectives. In other words it needs to be right.

Secondly, it must have the commitment of those who have to implement it. Many 'right' decisions fail dismally because they were not implemented effectively. This is particularly important where low motivation or a lack of support will undermine the desired results, as in sales or marketing programs.

As a general rule, if a decision requires the commitment of certain people in order to be successful, these people should be involved in the decision making process. The dilemma faced by franchisors is *how* to involve their franchisees in the decision making process when such involvement takes both valuable time and resources.

Experience shows that time and resources may be saved in the long run if there is open communication and involvement initially. Franchise Advisory Councils, discussed in the next chapter, provide a useful vehicle for such involvement.

Three types of decision making

There are broadly three types of decision making which exist on a continuum, with participative decision making at one end and directive at the other.

Franchisors need to decide which type of decision making they intend to use and then make it clear to those involved that this particular approach will be taken in a given situation. Difficulties often arise, not because the decision making process was flawed, but because people were confused about the process that was being used. The most common confusion occurs between participative and consultative decision making.

Participative decision making

Participative decision making involves the widespread participation of franchisees in what should be done, usually through discussions and forums. The implicit promise is that once agreement has been reached, the franchisor will implement the group's decision.

This process can be very time consuming and result in inappropriate decisions. In other words, people may have a high level of commitment to the outcome but the decision might not produce the desired results because of flawed assumptions or biased perspectives.

Participative decision making is seldom appropriate for significant strategic decisions because both objectivity and broad information are required. Moreover, the time lag in reaching agreement may result in opportunities being missed or threats not being addressed in time to prevent major problems from occurring.

This style is generally best kept for the following type of decisions:
- They are not significant to the future viability of the network.

- There is no urgency to arrive at a decision.

- Most people will probably agree with the outcome.

Consultative decision making

This involves consultation with franchisees on their thoughts and ideas. It usually has more to do with how a decision should be implemented rather than whether it should be implemented. In other words for tactical rather than strategic issues.

In this process franchisees may be invited to contribute their thoughts by survey, phone, email or through forums. The franchisor should make it clear that it will ultimately make the final decision, although it will take into account the information gathered from franchisees.

Directive decision making

Directive decision making involves the franchisor using their authority to make decisions about the network's future and how this decision will be implemented.

It is best used when resistance or a slowing down of the decision making process could threaten organisational success. For instance a franchisor may be forced to take a non-negotiable decision on an issue that is important to the larger survival of the group.

While directive decision making may be necessary or the most appropriate course to take in a situation, it can leave franchisees feeling alienated or cynical about whether they will be consulted in the future. Out of respect for franchisees, they should be informed about why and how the decision was made, including the information that was taken into account.

Another down side for a franchisor using directive decision making is that franchisees can be very unforgiving of too many mistakes. As a general rule if a franchisor stuffs up once on a major decision, franchisees will accept this if there is a good reason; twice they will be relentless in their questioning; three times and the franchisor will have great difficulty re-establishing its credibility.

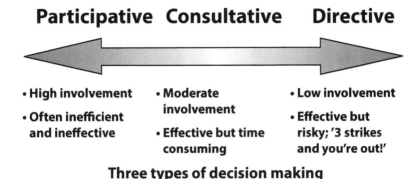

Three types of decision making

The Frustration Effect

Something I have frequently seen, which I call 'The Frustration Effect', arises when a franchisor wants to consult with franchisees, calls meetings, listens to their views and takes notes. So far so good.

However when the franchisor announces its decision there are some franchisees who disagree and become hostile and frustrated. "Why did you ask us for our opinion if you weren't going to take it on board?" they complain.

To prevent this from happening the franchisor should clearly communicate the following:

- By listening and consulting with you about your views, we are not necessarily agreeing with your views.

- Many of you will inevitably have differing views so it is unlikely that there will be one decision with which everyone will agree. This means some people may be unhappy with the final decision.

- The final decision will be made taking into account all the available information and views, and the long-term interests of everyone in our group.

Consultative decision making is useful where the decision is an important one and where resistance or lack of commitment over its implementation could result in problems. Consultation usually increases commitment, providing everyone understands the important ground rule:

Consultation does not mean agreement.

Which approach is best?

It is my belief that the consultative decision making process fits best with most franchise networks. Given the large number of decisions that normally need to be made and the fact that many of these require prompt attention, it is unrealistic and unwise to attempt to achieve agreement through a participative approach.

As for many of the minor day to day decisions, a directive approach can be the most appropriate.

Where franchise advisory councils or consultative groups have been established for regular meetings, it is important there is a clear understanding of which issues will be placed on the agenda for discussion and the type of decision making that will be used. It may be useful to ask the following questions:

- Is the franchisor wanting to discuss the issues with franchisees so that a collective decision can be reached to which everyone agrees? (participative)

- Is the franchisor genuinely wanting the ideas and views of the group so these can be taken into account when a final decision is to be made? (consultative)

- Does the franchisor merely want to inform the franchisees of its decision as well as the rationale and issues taken into account in reaching this decision? (directive)

Habits can be dangerous

Everyone has a preferred style of decision making. Some people are more controlling and directing in their style while others are more open and consultative.

If you are the type of person who likes to retain control and make quick decisions (as many franchisor executives are), you are likely to be most comfortable with a directive approach.

On the other hand if you prefer a team approach and have more of a facilitative management style you are most likely to be comfortable using a consultative or participative approach to decision making.

To be truly effective you need to put aside your habits and consider each situation according to its merits. You are most likely to achieve the best results if you make a conscious decision to use a particular type of decision making by analysing the needs of the situation rather than operating from habit or just working within your comfort zone.

There is not necessarily one right approach to making decisions. However the consequences may vary depending on the process you decide to use.

Knowledge struggles

Before closing this chapter, an issue that deserves a mention is what I call 'knowledge struggles'.

Sometimes a franchisee may disagree with the network's strategic direction and feel that he or she has a better grasp of the strategic environment than their franchisor. This can happen if the franchisee has held a high level corporate marketing or management position before joining the franchise network, or if someone they know and respect has made disparaging remarks about the franchisor's strategy. In such cases a knowledge struggle over 'who knows best' can ensue.

My advice in these cases is for both parties to step back from the posturing and consider the following questions:

- To what extent have I become embroiled in an ego battle? What is right is more important than who is right.

- What is motivating me to take this strong view? Am I trying to impress others? Am I angry because I can't get my own way?

- Do I really have the interests of the entire group at heart and have I considered the long-term implications of what I am proposing?

- Is the information on which I am basing my opinions, good quality, up to date objective information? Or is it based on fads or the views of others who may not have access to all the facts?

The franchisor in particular should be careful not to get on their high horse and take umbrage at a franchisee questioning their wisdom. If a strategy has been well thought through there should be no objection to sharing this logic with interested franchisees and inviting them to ask relevant questions.

There may come a point where enough discussion has taken place and, in the interests of getting on with the business, the parties will need to agree to disagree. If the franchisee feels so strongly about the issue that the relationship is under threat, there may be value in seeking a relevant consultant's opinion.

However leadership is about making decisions and, as I have repeated frequently in this book, the franchisor ultimately has this leadership responsibility. If a franchisee cannot accept this they may need to consider whether they are better operating independently, especially if they genuinely believe the franchisor's strategy is putting their business at risk.

In summary

There are no simple answers to the question of how decisions should be reached in a franchise system. Sometimes a more directive approach is better, while at other times consultation is essential — especially where the commitment of franchisees will be important for the successful implementation of the decision. In making decisions everyone needs to keep in mind that *what* is right is more important than *who* is right.

Action Tips:

- Where franchisees will be significantly affected by a particular decision, consider how they can best be involved in the decision making process in some way.

- Select people responsible for making decisions based on their maturity, objectivity, experience and calibre of thinking.

- Franchisors must maintain a strategic focus on the group's brand values, unique competitive advantage and core business. Decisive action should be taken if any of these areas starts to fragment.

- When making key decisions, embrace the philosophy, "The good of the many outweighs the needs of the few."

- Make it clear to people how Key decisions are to be made and ensure you do not give mixed messages that confuse consultative with participative decision making.

- Use the decision making process that best suits the situation rather than the one that best suits your personality.

- If you find yourself embroiled in a battle with someone over the best course of action, take some time out for reflection and question your real motives. Try looking at the situation from an outsider's point of view.

CHAPTER ELEVEN

How's Your Franchise Advisory Council?

The Franchise Advisory Council (FAC) embraces the view that franchisees, with their extensive front line experience and vested interest in the franchisor's decisions, can make a valuable contribution to the running of a franchise system. Because they seek to harness franchisee views in a systematic manner FACs are also a proven way of encouraging frank, honest communications between franchisees and franchisors. Given our research with thousands of franchisees shows only 61% believe there are avenues to contribute their ideas, FACs represent a powerful opportunity to build profitable partnerships.

Two types of FACs

There are broadly two types of franchise councils. The first is either established, or fully endorsed, by the franchisor. It will have significant franchisee involvement and is typically established to assist with the effective and harmonious operation of the franchise system for the benefit of franchisees and franchisor. Because this is the most common type, and is what people typically refer to when they talk of FACs, we will mainly focus on this type of FAC in this chapter.

However a second type, referred to as a Franchisee Association, also deserves mention.

These are usually born out of franchisee dissatisfaction and are established by franchisees with no franchisor involvement. They typically have a franchisee driven agenda and, because they are started in an adversarial manner with the goal of increasing franchisee power, they may take on a union mentality. Lawyers will often be involved, acting on behalf of the franchisees, which also tends to feed an adversarial approach.

Independent Franchisee Associations

The establishment of independent Franchisee Associations are often triggered when enough franchisees share one or more of the following concerns:

Security — concern over future security due to major changes being made to the franchise system. For instance a merger with another company, the franchisor company being sold or the non renewal of franchise agreements.

Franchisor viability — concern that the franchisor is financially unstable and thus may collapse leaving franchisees exposed. For instance, an administrator or receiver-manager may have been appointed.

Support — concern over a lack of relevant support to build franchisee profitability.

Marketing — a belief that marketing programs are inadequate or misguided. This can include advertising (eg. too much or too little), product range (eg. too broad or too narrow) or positioning (eg. wrong target market).

Rebates — concern that the franchisor is fleecing the system by taking significant supplier rebates that are not used for the benefit of franchisees and which are eroding the potential buying power benefits of the group.

Specific gripes — a specific gripe, usually over an issue that is impacting on franchisee sales or profitability. For instance promotions that are perceived as non-profitable.

Lack of input — concern that franchisees do not have adequate opportunities to contribute ideas that could improve the system.

Innovation — a perception that the franchisor is not undertaking sufficient entrepreneurial or innovative activity.

When a Franchisee Association starts to form, a franchisor has the choice of ignoring it by not recognising its status, or acknowledging it and trying to work with it in a positive way. The former approach typically promotes antagonism, the involvement of lawyers and constant posturing by both parties.

Some case studies show that, despite a rocky start, there can be a coming together of franchisees and franchisors for a common purpose if both parties maintain an ongoing dialogue and a commitment to interests, not positions. (See Chapter 9)

Where there is not agreement on the parameters of the Association or the Association is not endorsed by the franchisor, the relationship will inevitably become adversarial with destructive consequences for all parties. As is typical in these cases, the only winners are the lawyers.

My advice is that before establishing such an Association the franchisees meet with their franchisor to discuss why they feel their needs or interests are not being met and what alternatives might satisfy their needs.

Who pays

The costs of establishing and running a Franchise Advisory Council are typically shared in either of the following ways.

- Franchisees pay the costs. This can be in the form of a levy to cover the direct expenses of delegates. This is the case in about a third of FACs.

- The franchisor can pay the costs. This accounts for about another third of cases.

- Franchisees and franchisor can share the costs, which happens in about 20% of cases.

- The costs can be taken from the marketing fund, which tends to happen in about 10% of cases.

Common concerns of franchisors

Franchisors sometimes have concerns about establishing an FAC because they fear it might make franchisees too powerful or influential and they will thus lose control of the network. This type of thinking is misguided.

While FACs do increase the influence of franchisees this is not necessarily negative. What is negative is where franchisees try to gain greater control by banding together in a franchise association devoid of franchisor involvement. As mentioned earlier the negative communication which inevitably results in these reactive associations is usually damaging to the network. On the other hand, a proactive FAC established with the support of the franchisor can achieve many benefits for the entire group.

What the research tells us

International research shows that about 50% of franchise systems have some type of FAC and that the more mature a franchise system, the more likely it is to have one. Research also indicates the clear majority of franchisees and franchisors find them to be a positive initiative. There is however a bias for franchisors to see the FAC as more effective than the franchisees. Perhaps there is an element of wishful thinking here.

There is also evidence that franchisees and franchisors often have different perceptions on the role of the FAC, particularly with regard to power and influence. Where such a difference exists it will usually be that the franchisor sees the FAC as an advisory body with a focus on operational issues, while franchisees may see it as also having the power to make decisions on policy and strategy.

Clarity over structure and purpose is vital, as illustrated by the following story.

The runaway FAC

While setting up a new FAC, one of our clients was careful to establish clear guidelines for its decision making powers. With this in mind the charter stated the FAC was "to be a sounding board for new initiatives and strategies."

However the first meeting got off to a rocky start because the franchisees interpreted the charter to mean they were the Board and the franchisor was required to sound ideas off them for final approval! When this misunderstanding came to light, and the franchisees realised they did not have final veto over the franchisor's strategies, they felt somewhat hoodwinked. This is an ironic reminder that, because we all tend to hear what we want to hear, it pays to invest quality time clarifying expectations, especially on issues to do with purpose and powers.

Make it a joint exercise

The following guidelines provide the basis for a successful and constructive FAC. These should be worked out jointly by the franchisor and franchisees. Remember it is the franchisees' council so franchisor executives need to watch they do not fall into the trap of dominating meetings.

Most FACs choose to meet two to four times a year.

Structure, purpose and powers

Effective FACs usually have a written constitution or charter which guide their purpose, objectives, membership, code of conduct, frequency of meetings, how agenda items will be decided, the franchisor's role, costs and so on. Legal incorporation is unusual and is probably undesirable because of the costs involved, the legal liabilities of directors and state versus national incorporation issues.

There must be agreement on how decisions will be made and who holds what formal power. As mentioned earlier some franchise companies give the impression that their FAC has the power to make decisions when it is in fact an advisory body with no formal decision making power. In cases such as this FAC members can feel disempowered and will become cynical. Expectations and perceptions must be crystal clear on both sides. The objectives of the FAC should be clearly defined in writing.

Make sure objectives focus on the improvement of the whole network. Some examples of objectives are as follows:

- To improve communication between the franchisor and franchisees.
- To discuss problems with the aim of finding mutually beneficial solutions.
- To promote franchisee involvement in the development of new products and marketing programs.
- To increase franchisor/franchisee teamwork in serving customers.
- To maintain a positive focus for increasing the profitability of the franchisee and the franchisor.

In summary the ingredients to success seem to be clarity, consistency, a spirit of mutual respect and cooperation.

Membership

Rules of appointment to the FAC should be clearly understood. It is vital that members appreciate the commitment required and that they have an obligation to actively participate, not only in FAC meetings, but in all franchise systems events and activities so they have their finger on the pulse of what is happening.

Here are some recommendations regarding membership:

- A combination of franchisee elected members and franchisor appointed members can be a good idea.

- Membership should rotate so that only half the FAC changes at any one time. This helps to create consistency of purpose.

- Membership of the FAC should be restricted to franchisees or part owners as this maintains its status and influence. It may however be appropriate to invite non-members (eg. store managers or invited experts) to participate in parts of an FAC meeting or to join a sub-committee, for instance on a marketing sub-committee.

- Try to have as many experienced people as possible on the FAC.

- It should be a condition of membership that members are in good standing with the franchisor and most of the franchisees. There should be a clause that enables a member to be removed if they fail to attend meetings or retain the confidence of their fellow franchisees.

- Top management of the franchisor should participate in meetings as this signals that the FAC is regarded as important by the franchisor and not just a 'toothless tiger'.

Agenda

There does not appear to be any better or worse approach to how the meetings should be conducted providing they follow a planned agenda. This will prevent meetings from becoming 'gripe sessions' or 'waffle fests'. Have a definite cut-off date for agenda items to be submitted.

Items which do not comply with the objectives of the Council should not be discussed. For instance petty issues affecting a minority of stores should not be addressed. You may wish to specify this in the by-laws of the Council.

Always keep meetings constructive and enjoyable. If meetings run for more than one day it may be beneficial to use a more relaxed and neutral location.

Here are some topics commonly addressed in FAC meetings:

- Problems in communication within the network and suggestions for overcoming these.

- Ideas for coping with specific marketing challenges.

- Reviews of market research findings.
- Ideas on improving initial and ongoing training.
- Discussion on digital strategies.
- Improvements to benchmarking programs.
- Ideas on new products or services, raised either by the franchisor or franchisee.
- Ideas on new marketing programs or feedback on past programs.
- Difficulties or suggested improvements to accounting or reporting procedures.
- Suggestions for improving operational procedures.
- Specific people problems affecting the network.
- Introducing new initiatives into the franchise network.

Credibility

Ensure all franchisees and franchisor executives receive a report from every FAC meeting within a few days of the meeting. Everyone should be kept informed of the FAC's activities. Its credibility will depend on how effectively decisions are followed through. Franchisors need to keep in mind that the FAC should not be perceived as a tool to keep people compliant or act as a barrier to change.

The FAC needs to have status in the eyes of franchisees and the franchisor if it is to be effective. Members should be rewarded for their contribution through recognition at conferences and in newsletters. The FAC needs to be promoted as a vital part of the franchise system.

If the franchisor initiates the FAC it may take some time for it to gain the full trust and enthusiasm of the network. Franchisees may initially be sceptical or shy of involving themselves so the franchisor will need to take a patient and encouraging approach.

Preventing conflict

The FAC should enable a franchisor to stay in touch with any concerns or dissatisfaction which surface, enabling these to be dealt with before they fester and become nasty. Most serious conflicts begin with small dissatisfactions which remain unresolved. These then grow into more serious clashes. If the perception of conflicting needs continues a major crisis eventually emerges. Major conflicts do not happen overnight — they will have been brewing for some time.

Sharing power

In establishing an FAC the franchisor needs to accept they do not hold all the power in the network. Every time they sell another franchise opportunity they are giving away some power. It is the sharing of this power which makes the franchisor successful. The more the franchisee spreads his or her wings, the more the network grows.

The fine line the franchisor must walk is that it is giving away power while still needing to retain some control over how this power is used. The FAC can help to keep this balance of power in harmony. As mentioned earlier a simply but carefully worded charter, will help to guide and channel the FAC's power for the benefit of the whole system.

Predictors of successful FAC meetings

While FACs vary in their formality, our research indicates the level of formality is not a measure of success. Rather, the drivers of success appear to be fourfold:

1. A competent chairperson who keeps discussions focused on relevant issues, and is able to encourage open and constructive discussion. Whether the chairperson is a franchisor executive or a franchisee is irrelevant to the meeting's effectiveness, although for political reasons this may appear important.

2. The involvement of senior franchisor executives who maintain a genuine preparedness to listen and take action on legitimate issues.

3. Franchisee involvement by mature, commercially minded people who respect the rights and responsibilities of the franchisor and are motivated to enhance the value of the brand.

4. Agenda topics being of interest to both parties with the goal of finding mutual benefits.

Not surprisingly, the reasons why FACs fail to gain the support of franchisors or franchisees are the reverse:

1. Poorly chaired meetings that are allowed to degenerate into negative or distracted meanderings or where hidden agendas are allowed to fester.
2. Franchisors over-controlling meetings or giving lip service to listening, but not really engaging with the process.
3. Franchisees that are driven by personal or political agendas.
4. Agenda topics being of interest or benefit to only one party.

The role of the chairperson

Given the importance of the chairperson for an effective FAC, we will end this chapter with a summary of the chairperson's role.

Ensure meetings are run according to agreed guidelines. This includes intervening if discussions move outside the FAC charter or meeting guidelines.

Assist members to develop issues into agenda items. This will often require the chairperson to contact members prior to the meeting. They may sometimes need to suggest certain issues are not raised if these are outside the FAC's guidelines.

Facilitate constructive discussion. Lead the meeting toward consensus of views, bring discussions to a positive close, and encourage equal participation from all members.

Ensure minutes are clear and promptly distributed. Unclear minutes, particularly about decisions, can create later confusion and conflict. The chairperson may need to check from time to time in the meeting that the minute taker is accurately summarising key agreements or points.

More detailed strategies for improving the effectiveness of FACs, based on research by the Franchise Relationships Institute, can be found in the publication, *Making Franchise Advisory Councils Work,* available from www.franchiserelationships.com.

In summary

Franchise Advisory Councils are a tried and tested way for improving communication in a franchise system. In establishing the FAC everyone needs to accept that there will be some sharing of power. To prevent confusion over the real power an FAC has in influencing the strategy and policies of the franchise system, careful thought must be given to its purpose, processes and structures.

Action Tips:

- Be proactive in establishing an FAC once your franchise system has gone through its initial establishment phase.

- Franchisors and franchisees should discourage the establishment of associations that are devoid of franchisor involvement.

- Franchisors should resist the temptation of trying to control the FAC and allow franchisees at least equal say in how meetings are conducted.

- Put in the time up front to create a clear and agreed purpose for the FAC as well as good structures and processes for meetings. Ensure these are documented and adhered to.

- Run an annual review of the effectiveness of the FAC by polling everyone who has a stake in it.

- Be patient when first establishing an FAC and allow at least a year for teething problems to be sorted out.

- Remember the most important factor for success is a competent chairperson so select this person carefully. If necessary organise for them to have coaching or training in meeting management skills.

CHAPTER TWELVE
Maximising the Value of Field Visits

Field managers are employed by a franchisor to provide on-site consulting support to help franchisees grow their sales and profits, ensure the customer experience is being correctly delivered and facilitate a profitable working relationship. This chapter will show you how to leverage the power of these visits.

The dangers of habituation

In big business, consultants are regularly used to provide objective opinions and expert advice on how companies can improve their operations. It is an accepted fact that it is hard to be objective about a business when you are inside it. This means that management will often overlook significant opportunities and threats that are staring them in the face unless they are assisted to see these by someone with an outside perspective.

While small business people can seldom afford the input of consultants, most franchisees are fortunate in that they receive regular field visits that can provide them with such a fresh perspective on their business.

Retail blindness

The retailing industry has a term, 'retail blindness', to explain why standards often slip in a business. For instance, in many of the stores I visit I am struck by the out of date promotional posters on the walls, the products on the counters that don't make sense to me, the light globes that aren't working, the empty box sitting in the corner, and so on. I think to myself that the potential of the place is being wasted. Yet the owner and staff just don't see all this because they have become habituated to their environment.

Don't be a frog

It's a bit like putting a frog in a pot of cool water and then heating it. The frog can't sense the gradual increase in temperature and so passively stays where it is; and is slowly but surely cooked to death. Yet if you drop a frog in a pot of hot water it will immediately jump out to protect itself. Like frogs we are insensitive to the slow deterioration or small changes in our environment and, before we know it, we can be running our business in a way that is dangerously uncompetitive.

The field manager's role

The functions of the field manager usually fall into five areas:

Relating. Being a 'middleman' between franchisor and franchisee, communicating information back and forth.

Advising. Providing objective, expert advice on business, marketing or operational issues.

Coaching. Encouraging franchisees to achieve higher levels of performance and assisting them to get through motivational blocks.

Training. Upgrading the skills and knowledge of franchisees.

Inspecting. Ensuring standards are maintained.

The last of these can sometimes be contentious. However consistency lies at the heart of franchising and field managers have to ensure individual franchisees are not letting down the standards of the group.

To succeed in what is a very demanding role, field managers need to be people of high calibre with outstanding interpersonal skills. They also need high self-esteem to handle the criticism they must give and get as a part of their job.

Field visits are a costly investment so let's now look at how franchisees and franchisors can maximise their value.

Why visits may be wasted

Imagine that you employed a skilled and knowledgeable person to help you improve the profitability of your business. Then you equipped them with a car, smart devices and other paraphernalia so they could be as effective as possible. How would you feel if you then found this person driving around the streets aimlessly or sitting in a corner twiddling their thumbs?

Unfortunately this is what sometimes happens to field managers. There are commonly three reasons why the opportunities for positive and constructive field visits are lost.

Planning. Lack of planning on the part of the field manager or the franchisee means their time together is not used effectively. For instance the manager may not have a system to guide the visit or the franchisee may not have planned to have extra staff so he or she could be free during the visit.

Priorities. Franchisees or field managers not giving the field visit the priority it deserves. For instance franchisees may leave a field manager waiting for them to finish 'more important' business. Or field managers may get caught up with 'phone crises' that are unrelated to this franchisee during the visit.

Defensiveness. In the frog example above, if you were to tell the frog that he will cook and die if he doesn't get out of the pot he may laugh and say he is feeling quite comfortable thank you very much. And if you were to push the point, he would probably become agitated and ask you to politely mind your own business. Field managers often come up against the same response because their well-meaning feedback is construed as ill-informed criticism.

So what can field managers and franchisees do to avoid these pitfalls?

The six steps of effective field visits

While field visits are potentially one of the most positive and powerful points of contact for franchisor and franchisees they can also be stressful and threatening to both. After all, no one likes to be criticised or rejected. To reduce the stress of the field visit and make it a more productive experience for everyone I recommend the following simple model. Feedback from the field indicates that it works and I would encourage you to try it or to develop an approach that works for you.

You will see that this model breaks the field visit into six steps, starting with preparation and finishing with withdrawal.

Step 1 — Joint Preparation

Prior to the visit, the field manager should contact the franchisee to find out if there is anything specific he or she would like to cover during the visit. The manager should also inform the franchisee of any matters they want to address. A joint agenda of issues can then be developed and faxed or emailed prior to the visit.

This enables both parties to prepare for the visit and gather any information or materials needed for a productive discussion. Such preparation also enables franchisees to roster additional staff so they can be free to talk without being interrupted or distracted. It also prepares them for any new ideas the field manager might wish to present.

Step 2 — Initial Contact

The first ten seconds of the visit are vital and will set the tone for the rest of the meeting. If things get off on the right foot they will flow more smoothly.

Field advisers in particular should take time to prepare themselves mentally before entering the franchisee's premises so they are sensitive to what is happening in the business. You must avoid the temptation of barging into someone's business full of criticism or oblivious to what is going on around you.

This principle also applies to franchisees. It is off-putting for a field manager to be confronted with issues you are unhappy about the second they step foot in your business. Such an approach can undermine the effectiveness of the visit before it has even started.

One of the more seasoned field managers with Brumby's Bakeries, Ian O'Loughlin, used to tell me that when first entering a store he would pretend not to notice any burnt bread on the racks, crumbs on the floor or unkempt staff. He figured that this could all wait until he had established rapport with the franchisee or store manager. I think Ian had his priorities right.

At the other extreme I can remember accompanying our technical manager on a field visit and upon entering a particular store he picked up a slightly misshapen Vienna loaf from a display rack and threw it on the table in front of the store manager. "You call this a Vienna!?" he screamed for all to hear, including customers. To say this was not a productive visit would be an understatement. (This also raises the issue of managing pressure, covered in Chapter 14.)

Step 3 — Agree on Process

Field visits are ideally a collaborative exercise. So first review how long the visit will last, what will be covered (which should be outlined in the agreed agenda) and the process to be used.

These first three steps are a bit like the initial work we must do to get a satisfactory result when renovating a room. Most of our time will be taken sanding and preparing the walls so, when we are ready to apply the paint, we know it will stick and look good.

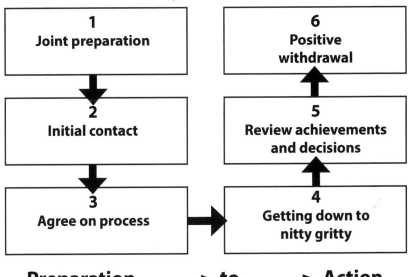

Preparation – – – ➤ to – – – ➤ Action
The Six Steps of Effective Field Visits

Step 4 — Nitty Gritty

Now you are ready to 'roll up your sleeves' and get involved with the items on your agenda. It is possible that either party will get defensive, particularly the franchisee, if issues of compliance are being discussed. The skills of active listening discussed in earlier chapters will be a great asset in keeping the communication flowing.

Step 5 — Review Achievements

Towards the end of the visit when the field manager has completed the various checklists and the agreed items on the agenda have been dealt with, a review process should be followed. Go over what has been achieved during the visit, discuss the outcomes and make a note of things that need to be acted on by both parties. This will not only provide an opportunity to clarify any areas of uncertainty, it will also give you a greater sense of satisfaction that the visit has accomplished something.

If the visit has been emotionally charged, now is the time for both parties to re-establish a sense of trust and commitment for the future. Keep the big picture in mind — what you are all here for — long term prosperity and success.

Step 6 — Positive Withdrawal

Visits should end on a positive note. How this visit finishes sets the tone for the start of the next. If either person has been brash, pushy or obnoxious the next visit is unlikely to go well because there will be a residual resentment that will colour the relationship.

Field managers should also not 'hang around' at the end of the visit as the franchisee will inevitably have things he or she will want to resume doing.

Common mistakes made by field advisers

- Dropping in unannounced on a franchisee with no clear purpose. This can be disruptive and distracting for the franchisee or their staff.

- Instructing franchisee staff members without the permission of the franchisee.

- Making provocative off-the-cuff remarks that get a franchisee's back up.

- Being critical of their franchisor colleagues (for instance if the franchisee brings up an issue concerning another member of the franchisor team).

- Allowing other pressures or crises to intrude into the visit, for instance taking phone calls.

- Being overly chummy with franchisees or treating the visit as a social call.

- Not following up on promises and commitments agreed to during the visit.

- Letting the visit drag on for too long by not maintaining a sense of focus and urgency.

Common mistakes made by franchisees

- Not planning to be available, so the field adviser is left waiting and wastes his or her time.

- Being rude or difficult to deal with, for instance as a way of punishing the field adviser for past 'transgressions' by the franchisor.

- Saying that you want more or better quality help but not being clear or specific on this.

- Not appreciating the strategic or business development focus of the field adviser. For instance wanting them to serve customers or do operational work for you.

- Allowing business or personal pressures to intrude on the visit and thus becoming negative or distracted.

- Being overly chummy and treating the visit as a social call.

- Being secretive or non-forthcoming with business information, thus restricting the level of quality input the adviser can give.

- Not following up on promises and commitments agreed to during the visit.

How to maximise the value of field visits

Do reviews together. Regular reviews should be done together so that both parties understand what action is needed. This will avoid any possibility of a breakdown in communication.

Try reversing the roles. Occasionally you should both consider what it would be like if you were on the other end of the visit, ie. what sort of person would you each like to deal with?

Deal with personality clashes. Personality clashes will occur from time to time. If an issue gets personal and you can't work it out, an objective third person should be used to help resolve the situation. It may be that things have been said which have resulted in bruised egos and it is better for a different field adviser to service this franchise in the future.

Be clear on the purpose of visits. Field staff should always be clear in their own mind as to why they are making contact with a franchisee and what they want to achieve from the visit.

Be regular and consistent with contact. Regular contact between franchisor and franchisees has been shown to be a significant contributor to the success and high standards of the best franchise systems. It is also important that franchisees feel the franchisor is consistent in its standards and approach.

Make visits a pleasant experience. Be sure to courteously greet and farewell each other. Neither party should feel embarrassed or apprehensive if there were to be another visit tomorrow!

Provide written follow-up. Visits should always be recorded in writing. Usually some sort of franchisee contact form will be used for this purpose. Visits may become a contentious issue at some time in the future and, if so, it is useful for both parties if there is a written record.

Maintain a sense of urgency. This helps to keep everyone's concentration high as well as ensuring the visit does not drag on unnecessarily.

The early months

On first joining a network a franchisee may have doubts or fears about their ability, about the location, about the product or service, and so on. Field managers can help to allay these fears through sensible advice and being available when they are needed.

The first 90 days are particularly critical as the new franchisee gets on his or her feet. Better to provide too much support during this important time than risk feelings of neglect that can sow the seeds of later dissatisfaction. Also the habits which the franchisee establishes in this initial period will be very difficult to break later.

Weekly contact with the franchisor is recommended during the first three to six months of a franchisee's operation. This may not always be face to face. Structured phone calls, online discussions and emails can also be a source of effective support.

Different philosophies of field reviews

As part of a franchisor's support procedures there should be a system whereby franchisees are regularly reviewed on a range of specific criteria. For instance many franchisors have major quarterly, half-yearly or annual reviews. Meaningful and relevant checklists should guide these performance reviews. Checklists should also be very specific in their wording, particularly where standards are concerned.

There are different philosophies and approaches regarding how formal these reviews are and the extent to which franchisees are involved in the process.

Here are some examples:

- Franchisees are invited to conduct their own review on themselves, using a checklist provided by the franchisor.

- Franchisees review each other's businesses.

- Franchisees conduct the review with a field adviser and negotiate on what is and is not acceptable.

- 'Mystery customers' are used to purchase products and services and secretly review the standards of the franchisee and report back to the franchisor.

- A team of franchisor inspectors descends unannounced on the franchisee to check they are operating up to required standards.

Rather than provide one recipe, I encourage you to develop an approach that is most suitable for your franchise system and culture. Whatever the method used, remember that the purpose of the review is to build stronger and more profitable businesses, not to give franchisees a hard time.

Some useful questions

In deciding on the best approach ask yourself these questions:

- What is the purpose of the review?

- Who is going to pay for the review?

- How do we ensure everyone involved gets good value for money?

- What resources do we have at our disposal and what is the best way for us to use these?

- What is our customer promise and how can we best ensure that franchisees are delivering on this?

- How are we going to define and measure standards that are and are not acceptable?

- How can we encourage the review to be valued by franchisees?

- How directive do we want to be? And what are the likely consequences of this?

- How can we reduce the stress and inconvenience of the review for everyone?

- What approach best fits our culture?

Reviewing franchisee competence

While most reviews focus on the physical and financial aspects of the business such as cleanliness, merchandising and profitability, I am a great believer in also measuring the human dimension — franchisee competence. Competencies are simply attributes that contribute to the franchisee's ability to run a profitable business and satisfy customers.

Although competencies are the things that will ultimately drive a franchisee's success, many companies shy away from measuring them because they believe it is too difficult, which it is not. We will cover this issue in more detail in Chapter 16. If you are interested in knowing more about measuring franchisee competencies you might also like to visit www.franchiserelationships.com.

Why criticism hurts

Golda Meir was reported to have said that when it comes to criticism most people embrace the philosophy that it is better to give than to receive.

The reason we are sensitive to receiving criticism is that it tends to bruise our ego. When criticism is given for the wrong reasons or in a destructive way, for instance out of envy, anger or revenge, it can also undermine our confidence and self-esteem — both important for happiness and psychological wellbeing. It makes sense then that no one wants to be criticised.

The fact is however that field advisers are frequently in a position where they do need to give criticism about a franchisee's standards or performance.

Criticism is not always a dirty word, it is how you give it that counts. When given for the right reasons and in a respectful way, it can actually resolve feelings of stress and anxiety because people know where they stand. Being able to criticise in a positive and open way can also promote trust and honesty.

A more acceptable term for criticism is 'feedback' so let's use this as we explore some practical ways of giving and receiving criticism.

Giving feedback

Be clear on your motives

If your feedback is motivated out of anger, frustration or impatience it will almost certainly have negative repercussions for you and the other person. If you are unsure of your motives ask yourself this question:

"Am I trying to punish this person?"

If you are, you are probably criticising for the wrong reasons. The purpose of feedback is to improve another person's performance, not to judge or punish them.

Keep your composure

Clear thinking is important. Emotions such as anger and fear fog up our thinking and get in the way of clear communication. Try to remain relaxed and composed when giving feedback.

Depersonalise the feedback

In the franchise setting policies and standards should be stated in manuals and checklists. Field advisers can refer back to these standards as a way of depersonalising their comments. Moving the relationship back to formal roles and responsibilities is also an effective way of avoiding sticky personality clashes. For instance:

"Angelo, in my role as field adviser I am responsible for ensuring that standards are maintained. Because of this, I need to talk with you about the state of your van, more specifically the paintwork. Is it okay if we talk about this?"

Give encouragement and recognition

People tend to work best if they receive regular positive feedback as to how they are performing. If a person has made an effort and achieved a result in the right direction — even if the end target has not yet been met — it is better to give encouragement and recognition for what has been achieved than to criticise for what has not. Psychological research has repeatedly shown that focussing and building on achievements improves long-term performance while being critical and focusing on what has not been achieved has the opposite effect.

Focus on the behaviour

When giving feedback, concentrate on the behaviour or the actions of the person, not on the person themselves. Also talk about how the other person's action affects you or other people rather than on what you think about them. You might also point out how you would prefer them to behave in the future. So instead of saying, "Julie, you make my life a misery — I can't stand you", you could say something like this.

"Julie, when you stood up at the meeting last week and criticised me in front of everyone it was a real downer for the whole group. I also found it extremely embarrassing. In future I'd prefer it if you spoke to me privately if you have any problems about my visits to your store."

Don't beat around the bush

Sometimes we get caught up worrying about how a person will react to our feedback and so we beat around the bush or avoid being specific or direct. The irony is that the more we focus on our fear of their reaction, the more likely our fears will be realised. Better to concentrate less on the person and more on the issue at hand and why it is important.

If the person does react and get angry, point out that your intention was not to upset them and that you are just providing information that could be useful to them. It is possible that a person will get angry because of other concerns they have which have nothing to do with you or the issue being discussed.

Address recurring problems

If you have to address recurring problems follow these steps:

- Firstly raise the fact that you need to talk with the person about a recurring problem. Be factual and straightforward in your approach. Check if here and now is okay to talk.

- Then describe the problem situation and its impact on you or others. Suggest what you would like to see happen.

- Ask them how they feel about what you have said and whether they think it's reasonable. Then listen carefully to their perspective on the situation.

- Agree on a solution and an action plan; and don't forget to follow this up.

- Finally, thank them for taking the time to talk with you.

Receiving feedback

If you are on the receiving end of feedback that you perceive is critical or unfair, a range of psychological protection mechanisms will start to kick in. These might include:

- Feeling indignant or angry.
- Thinking that the other person is a fool.
- Looking for faults in the other person's logic.
- Wanting to attack and criticise them.
- Having the urge to break contact with them (eg. physically leave the situation or hang up the phone).
- Wanting to change the subject.
- Losing concentration and thinking about other things.
- Feeling guilty and ashamed for being such an incompetent idiot.

While these are natural reactions, the question is whether they are going to help you to achieve your goals. Here are a few things you can do to regain control of yourself, and become a participant in the conversation rather than a victim of it.

Ask why

Ask the person to clarify why they are giving you this feedback. What are they hoping will come out of the conversation? If their motive is to punish you and make you feel guilty or bad, this question is likely to stop them in their tracks and change the tone of the discussion to a more positive one.

If their motive is to genuinely assist you in some way, you can say something like this.

"Dave, I appreciate you spending the time to tell me about this. If we are to achieve something worthwhile from this conversation it would be better for me if..."

You might then suggest they could talk more slowly or softer; or ease off a little on the moralising; or that it would be better to have the conversation in a more private environment; or that having these things in writing first and then talking about them later would work better — or whatever.

Name the process

If you are getting defensive and finding the conversation unpleasant, you can state what is happening and then wait for the other person to respond. For instance:

"Nicole, what's happening here is that you are giving me this feedback because you want to be helpful but I am actually finding it unpleasant and starting to feel defensive."

Then stop and listen. You may be pleasantly surprised to find that this simple approach leads to a very positive conversation about the process of communication which will usually clear the air and make room for a more productive discussion.

Take a break

Ask if you can take a break for a few minutes, for instance to visit the bathroom. Use this time to settle down, focus on the bigger picture and think about how this feedback could be relevant to helping you achieve your goals.

Be grateful

Treat the feedback as valuable, free information. The fact that this person is bothering to put him or herself out to give you their message is a sign they care. This will require you to take a different perspective on the conversation and treat it more like the gift it is rather than as a punishment — a gift that will help you to become stronger, wiser and more competent.

Get curious

Instead of passively accepting what is being said, dig deeper into what they are saying almost joining with the person to really understanding what is wrong and how it can be improved. Treat the process as one of joint research and enquiry on how you can run a better business.

Setting goals for improved performance

Franchising is about franchisors and franchisees working together to maximise the performance of their respective businesses. Performance will always be best when both parties have set specific goals. However telling a franchisee that he or she must aim at certain goals is a useless exercise. He or she must recognise the importance of the goal and have a personal commitment to it.

The best way of reaching a joint goal is by talking through why it is important and, where necessary, pointing out the consequences of not addressing the issue. For instance if specific things are not attended to, this may lead to a drop in profits and future headaches for the franchisee or franchisor.

The best goals comply with the following SMART acronym:

Specific. Spell out exactly what you are talking about. Leave minimal room for interpretation. Standards are useful here.

Measurable. Goals that can be measured are more motivating because there is a clearer sense of when they have been achieved.

Agreed upon. The people who are responsible for carrying out the actions must feel a degree of commitment or no action is likely to be taken.

Realistic. Given the current circumstances, is the goal achievable?

Time Limit. Having a date to work toward creates urgency and activity.

For example, continuing an earlier example about Angelo and his van, rather than agreeing that Angelo will do his best to clean up his van, a better goal would be:

By September 24th to have the van complying with the image standards of the company as defined in section 17 of the operations manual.

This makes life a lot easier for both parties because there is now minimal room for misunderstandings. We will return to the issue of goal setting in Chapter 15.

In summary

Well constructed field visits can significantly improve business performance. However tangible results will only be achieved if field managers are of a high calibre, the visits are well planned and everyone gives them the priority they deserve.

Action Tips:

- Select field managers carefully according to their interpersonal skills and ability to assist franchisees to grow their business.

- Preplan visits so that potential distractions such as phone calls are avoided.

- Maintain a sense of urgency throughout the visit.

- Structure goals according to the SMART formula where possible.

- Follow up on the actions to which you have committed.

- Incorporate a review of a franchisee's management development needs into your yearly field visit schedule.

- Regularly assess the effectiveness of visits by working through the questions on page 123.

- When giving feedback be objective, encouraging, solution focussed and direct.

- Welcome constructive feedback and ask for reasons if you think the feedback is unfair.

- Field managers — do not 'drop in' on franchisees without having a clear purpose for your visit.

- Franchisees — be open with your business information and respect the strategic role of field managers, ie. don't expect them to work in your business for you.

- Invite 'outsiders' to regularly visit the business and give you their honest observations. Fellow franchisees, customers or even friends can fulfil this role.

CHAPTER THIRTEEN
Succeeding Through Change

Technology is changing, the nature of families is changing, life-styles and working patterns are changing, the global economy is changing and government legislation on franchising continues to change. So it is not surprising that change continues to be a topical issue.

In such a dynamic environment, our success will be largely determined by how well we manage and communicate this change, especially in a franchise system where the needs of customers, franchisees and the franchisor must be met.

In this chapter we will firstly discuss the business challenges that inevitably face a franchise system as it grows. Then we will look at some of the ongoing external changes in the market that franchisees and franchisors must face together if they are to survive. Finally I will suggest ways that those on the receiving end of change can better cope.

The birth of a franchise system

Franchisor companies often start as 'lean and mean' enterprises with a small multi-skilled management team. The first few years inevitably test the limits of the founder's perseverance and dedication to their concept and the franchising way of doing business.

If the commitment of the franchisor remains strong, the concept is sound and franchisee profit levels are good the network will grow, often rapidly.

Along with this growth comes recognition by the business community and customers. The franchisor management team naturally becomes proud of its success and a sense of invulnerability may develop.

However there comes a time where the franchisor is forced to take stock of its achievements and review its operations. This may be forced upon it by internal management problems, unexpected competition or a realisation that franchisees are not as profitable as was assumed.

From family to corporation

There will typically be a period of 'navel gazing', restructuring and attempts to bring about significant internal change, often with the help of an external consultant. The aim of this change is usually to improve the profitability of both franchisees and the franchisor.

Following a lot of planning with much trial and error the franchisor will eventually establish an appropriate corporate structure with suitable management controls and information systems. Not surprisingly, this transition from a 'family' to a 'corporate' culture is not without its difficulties. If not well managed, this transition can take years and represent a significant threat to the company's survival.

Barriers to building successful corporations

Here are some important issues to consider during such periods of change.

Be open to learning

Unhelpful rituals and procedures regarding 'how we do things around here' often need to be challenged and replaced with an attitude of openness to change and continual learning.

Management stress

Because management changes usually have to be implemented on the run it is often an incredible balancing act maintaining stability and consistency on the one hand, while introducing new people and new ways of doing things on the other. This can be very stressful for a management team.

Franchisee confusion

Franchisees will inevitably be observing management changes from the sidelines. They may complain that they are confused about who is doing what and that they don't know who to talk to any more. There can be a fear that their friendly franchisor is turning into an impersonal corporation. As the level of franchisee anxiety increases, the quality of communication typically decreases creating a breeding ground for rumours, mistrust and even disputation.

Internal politics

Internal politics may also increase for a time as people find they are required to let go of old ways of doing things, move out of their comfort zone and perhaps even give up their established power base. For instance long standing franchisees who once yielded considerable influence over their franchisor may now feel left out of things. If internal politicking occurs at senior management or board levels, the organisation can become particularly vulnerable.

Leadership focus

The franchisor-founder may need to let go of the day to day running of the business and allow someone fresh to take the reins in a general management capacity. As a result of all these leadership changes, the organisation might for a time find itself unfocussed, allowing competitors to gain a foothold in its hard earned market share.

Loss of operational expertise

As the company establishes its new corporate focus strategic excellence can be elevated above operational excellence, which is a big mistake. A franchisor must never forget that the ultimate success of its system lies in operational excellence. Yet during the previous changes the operational knowledge of the company may have become lost, usually because key people have moved on. Careful documentation of how things are done can prevent this to some extent.

Alienation

As organisations grow and bring in new people many of the old traditions will be swept aside or lost. The biggest challenge for the franchisor as it moves into the corporate phase is to retain the good things about its previous culture. It can be useful to keep the Franchise Advisory Council in the picture as this will enhance commitment and understanding of the organisation's evolving strategy. Group planning sessions and team building processes can also work wonders in re-establishing a sense of cohesion and a shared vision for the future.

From corporate success to bureaucracy

History teaches us that all great empires eventually crumble. For whatever reasons — laziness, arrogance or even corruption — a certain complacency eventually creeps into most large organisations.

As a franchise company evolves into a corporation the drive for learning, continuous improvement and effectiveness can be replaced by a tendency to predictability, orderliness and efficiency. Welcome to the bureaucracy.

Large well-established franchise systems of this type can continue to prosper for years, especially if they are leaders in their market sector. However all markets eventually change. Customers decide they want a new type of product or service. Competitors arrive on the scene with exciting new offers and soon the profitability of both franchisor and franchisee decline. Inevitably the shareholders and stakeholders of a bureaucratic franchisor will put their foot down and a painful process of reinvention will occur.

If the franchise company fails to successfully make the necessary changes it may fold or be sold. Perhaps a group of franchisees or entrepreneurial managers will band together to pick up the pieces with fresh ideas and a new approach.

External market challenges

In addition to the above internal challenges there are external social and economic changes that require franchise systems to be adaptable and flexible in the way they do business. For instance, the nature of families is changing, as are lifestyles, working patterns and business practices. Technology and globalisation are driving many of these changes.

All this has serious implications for franchise companies which will need to continually adapt if they are to remain competitive and relevant to their customers. For instance most franchise systems regularly have to address the following:

- Introducing new products or services. Customers expect excitement and interest — not the same old stuff. New technology or the pricing policies of competitors may also force you to change your core products.

- Providing customers with better value for money, usually better quality at more competitive prices. Globalisation is forcing companies to continually introduce new methods of delivering better value to their customers.

- Upgrading premises, facilities or vans so the corporate image projected to the customer remains fresh and relevant to their needs.
- Opening longer hours. People are time poor and want to be able to shop when it suits them — day or night, weekday or weekend.
- Changing the way goods are distributed, for example providing customers with the option of purchasing products or services online from a central website. This can create resentment by franchisees who feel their franchisor is competing against them.
- Introducing new systems for monitoring performance and benchmarking productivity against peers and competitors. To remain competitive, accurate, up-to-date information is essential.

The trends are clear. Your franchise system will most definitely be touched by significant change and whether you are a member of the franchisor team or a franchisee, you will need to adapt to this change at both the business and personal levels.

Why people resist change

While people tend to have a natural curiosity to learn and seek new information that will lead to development and growth, there is also a part that seeks certainty and comfort. This is the part that resists change. Here are some reasons why we tend to resist change:

Control — we feel we don't have enough control or power over our situation.

Security — we feel insecure or unsure of what to expect.

Habit — we find it difficult to change established habits.

Vitality — we feel worn out or lacking the energy required.

Loss — we think we are losing something of value, for example security, competence, relationships, sense of direction, territory.

Personality— some of us are more adaptable than others.

Cynicism — we don't trust the competence or intentions of those driving the change.

The myth of painless change

There are basically two types of change. The change we choose and the change that chooses us. While the former can be motivating and exciting, the latter is at best challenging and at worst frightening. When people are asked to express how they feel when change chooses them they usually describe it as an intensely unpleasant experience. For example the following words are commonly used:

"shocked ... confused ... anxious ... angry ... frustrated ... cynical... betrayed ... horrified ... lost"

Yet there is a myth that change can be clean and painless if people just 'get on with it'. The fact is that working with change means working with some mess, frustration, chaos and confusion. This is inevitable. The Chinese saying "Out of great confusion comes bliss, certainty and progress" is relevant here.

At the deeper parts of an organisation lie the values, identity and assumptions which members of the organisation hold. If these are threatened, strong feelings of loss or rage can be evoked.

Emotional reactions to change

When people are on the receiving end of change, they typically move through specific emotional stages in the following sequence.

Fear

Initially fear or anxiety might be aroused. People often deal with this by pretending the change is not happening or if they ignore it, it will go away. In extreme situations feelings of fear can turn into a sense of paranoia about the organisation's real motives for the proposed change.

Sadness

Feelings of loss or despair can then occur as people begin to think about what they may be losing or missing out on. They may also romanticise about how simple business and life used to be before the change.

Anger

Resentment and anger may follow as people either openly or covertly challenge the legitimacy of the change. Conflict is common at this point as people try to turn back the clock.

Helplessness

As people start to accept the inevitability of the changes a sense of confusion, helplessness or doubt about their capacity to cope or adjust can overwhelm them. At this stage people's motivation temporarily drops as they try to get their heads around how they will cope.

Excitement

Finally, as their confidence and understanding grows, people will start to embrace the changes and make them their own. At this stage a resurgence of motivation occurs as people set new goals and get on with things.

Why change programs fail

Change is usually driven by shifts in the market that in turn necessitate change within the franchise system. However franchisees don't always understand this and may feel that the franchisor is trying to punish them or deliberately make life difficult. Communicating clear messages that address people's concerns and make them feel understood is undoubtedly one of the greatest challenges faced by the franchisor.

Research indicates that up to 80 per cent of change programs do not achieve their objectives because of poor implementation. Somewhere between the formation of the strategy and its implementation things go wrong. Senior management usually has its own view of what has gone wrong which typically is different from the franchisees or the people working in the field.

Research also indicates that ineffective top leadership and poor interpersonal and communication skills by leaders are the major reasons why most change programs fail. It appears that, rather than working with the actual feelings and issues faced by people in the field, franchisors frequently work on the issues that they believe are important. Furthermore, franchisors who see change as being resisted may push franchisees or their field advisers to accept the change by sweeping aside their concerns as unnecessary. The result is that people stop communicating or pretend that all is well when it is not.

Anticipate emotional reactions

As long as a franchisor remains 'out of sync' with the experience of its franchisees it will fail to gain the commitment it needs. Instead there is likely to be:

- increased stress and conflict between people

- low morale, apathy and lack of support for meetings
- outrageous rumours and passive sabotaging of projects
- reluctance by franchisees to try new initiatives

In summary, while senior franchisor executives may have the strategic issues right, if they fail to anticipate the emotional reactions of the people in the field or at the coalface, the change program will at best falter and at worst fail dismally in reaching its objectives.

A franchisor that is committed to the long-term performance of its franchise system needs to foster the development of strong people management skills in its management team and its franchisees. I am talking here about many of the skills covered in this book such as active listening, conflict management and group facilitation.

BOHICA

A large New Zealand company asked me for feedback on how it could improve its retail franchise network. As part of the project we organised a series of focus groups with franchisees, store managers and franchisor executives.

The eight people in the store manager's group had been with the company for the longest and, although they were polite and chatty, I had a feeling they were not telling me what they really thought. Eventually I said "Look, this group is very important because you have all been here the longest and probably have the most insight into how this company really operates. But I feel you are holding back something from me."

There were big grins all around the room. (I find that people usually smile when you hit on the truth.)

"Well Greg", they said. "It's nothing personal but we think this is just another BOHICA."

"BOHICA?" I asked, thinking it must be some sort of Maori word.

"Yes.. .Bend Over Here It Comes Again."

When the laughing subsided, I asked them to tell me about their BOHICA experiences. It turned out that for the past ten years the company had been wheeling in a succession of consultants each with their own pet hobby horse. While some of these costly initiatives had delivered value, many were fads and some had been demoralising and time consuming. No wonder they were cynical. In their view I was just another BOHICA peddler.

Dealing with cynicism is probably the most challenging task of any executive group trying to introduce new initiatives into a network — especially if franchisees or managers have already been exposed to over-hyped change programs that were driven top down, failed to take into account their input or ideas and failed to deliver the promised results.

Are you a hardy or a softy?

With the growing pace of change, it is not surprising that change has been identified as one of the greatest sources of stress and pressure in business today.

Psychologists who study people's reactions to change have found that there are three important personality characteristics that distinguish people who cope well and remain healthy, from those who succumb to stress. These are called the characteristics of the 'hardy personality'.

A sense of control rather than a feeling of powerlessness

Hardy people feel they have a sense of control over events which happen to them. They look for the reasons why things have happened and then seek out ways of doing something about the situation. This is sometimes called having an 'internal locus of control'. The alternative is to feel we are victims of life and the subject of forces over which we have no control. Some tips for enhancing this sense of control are given below and in the next chapter.

Interpreting change as a challenge rather than a threat

Hardy people accept that change is a normal part of life and accept this change as a challenge rather than a threat. They focus on new opportunities and creative possibilities. Rather than looking at what they might be losing they look for what they might be gaining, either in a material sense or as valuable experience. To improve our hardiness to stress we need to be prepared to bend a little and accept that situations do not always have black or white answers.

A willingness to get involved rather than sit on the fence

Hardy people are comfortable about committing themselves to their work, their family, their values and their own sense of wellbeing. They don't hold back and they don't allow change to alienate them. Rather than trying to keep events and changes at arm's length, we are better to find ways of involving ourselves and of understanding how the changes will affect us. In other words we should take an active role in the change and talk about 'us' and 'we' rather than 'them' and 'you'.

Making friends with change

How we feel at a particular time is not an accident of nature. Feelings often result from habits of thinking. Therefore, if we shift how we **think** about change, it can alter how we **feel** about change.

The table below has tips for thinking differently about change, particularly when we are on the receiving end.

This chapter has touched on the inevitability of change and the complex issues associated with managing change in an organisational environment. Of one thing we can all be sure: the level of skill and intelligence of franchisors and franchisees in responding to these changes will impact heavily on their personal well being and their ability to remain competitive.

Instead of thinking this ...	Try thinking this ...
It might be fine in theory but it won't work in my situation ...	Maybe I can adapt it to suit my situation.
It might be a good idea but I haven't got the time to use it...	If I give it a high priority I will find the time.
I shouldn't rush into this — best to think about it and see what happens ...	If I keep putting things off my business will stay the same. Is this what I really want?
If we try these ideas we are sure to run into heaps of problems ...	It's normal to have problems when trying something new. So we will fix them.
Things are not that bad that I need to make the drastic changes suggested ...	Why wait till things get worse? It makes better sense to act now while I can.
What they are talking about does not apply to me ...	As long as I am in this group, what they are talking about does apply to me.

Table adapted from the work of Dr Cliff Banning, IMC.

In summary

All franchise companies face inevitable internal and external challenges that require them to change how they operate. Whether these changes achieve their goals depends on the willingness of top leadership to embrace good communication practices and the willingness of franchisees to remain open and adaptable.

Action Tips:

- Franchisors should review their strategy, structures and business processes at least every two years with the help of an external facilitator or consultant.

- Quick and ruthless changes may need to be made if the franchisor or franchise system is found to be significantly out of step with the needs of the market.

- Keep franchisees informed during periods of internal restructuring. The FAC can serve a useful purpose here.

- Do not allow key people to leave the organisation until their operational knowledge has been recorded, systematised or passed onto a suitable person.

- Hold regular briefing sessions and forums to share information on market changes and the potential implications for everyone's business.

- Plan for some chaos and emotional turmoil during periods of change.

- Franchisors — train your executives in the interpersonal skills necessary to manage people through the emotional stages of change.

- Franchisees — maintain an open mind to the relevance of the change to your business's success.

CHAPTER FOURTEEN
Beating Stress and Achieving Life Balance

There was a time when the franchisor company I was working for hit a number of operational and financial crises all at once and was at risk of going into liquidation. We responded with some serious 'belt tightening' and I agreed to take on several roles, including national marketing and operations, and some local field management.

After six months of non-stop 'fire fighting' I remember one day pulling over to the side of the road feeling totally exhausted and despondent. I was in fact suffering from a mild case of burnout, which was also causing a range of physical health problems.

I realised that if I did not quickly pull myself out of this hole I would not only be a burden to myself and my family, but that because of my critical role, I could very well be the final nail in our corporate coffin.

Much of what is contained in this chapter is based on my experience applying common sense mental and physical disciplines to get my life back into shape. I am pleased to report that we also managed to get the company back into good shape and today, although I am no longer involved, it is one of the most prosperous franchise systems in Australasia.

Failure on the outside

In the previous chapter we learned that many people are finding the uncertainty and ambiguity of life today very stressful. While they want to slow down, take a break, be less materialistic, spend more time with their kids and the people they care about, the reality is that life is getting faster, more complex and more pressured.

This chapter is particularly important because, unless you personally learn to keep your head and maintain your health in all this pressure, there is no way you will be able to sustain your success.

Every business failure I have seen has been preceded by a gradual disintegration of confidence on the inside. The person has simply been unable to maintain the courage, focus, vitality and the will to keep going in the face of adversity. In other words, failure on the outside often results from failure on the inside. So let's go within and find out a bit more about what makes us tick.

Franchisor stress

Most franchisor executives bring a certain zeal, commitment and idealism to their work with their plans of creating large networks of profitable and happy franchisees. However high workloads combined with the continual emotional strains of the franchise relationship can take its toll.

Faced with the pressures of expansion and the challenge of sustaining a network of demanding franchisees who are working their way through The Franchise E-Factor (see Chapter 8), franchise executives can easily find themselves feeling browned off and emotionally worn down. Indeed it is not unusual for franchise executives to confide to colleagues that, in retrospect, if they had known that being a franchisor was going to be so hard, they would not have expanded through franchising.

Field advisers also often take on the trials and tribulations of their franchisees as if they were their own problems. Many find the feelings of responsibility and commitment to so many franchisees quite daunting.

Franchisee stress

Franchisees also face constant pressure on a number of levels. There is the emotional pressure of having one's life savings on the line and a constant stream of demands from customers, staff and the franchisor. Everyone wants something from you! These demands are often combined with the uncertainty of weekly sales fluctuations and the frustration of dealing with ever rising expenses and dwindling margins.

As a result, franchisees can wear themselves down working long hours, adjusting to the demands of their business and becoming frustrated or dissatisfied with the relationship they have with their franchisor. They may then become complacent about the standards of their business, cynical about the benefits of being in the franchise, rude or indifferent to customers and generally non-communicative.

Any franchisee who is serious about their business success cannot ignore the issue of stress. In a large and extensive study of small business owners, Professor Alan Williams from the University of New England concluded that stress is likely to be the major cause of small business failure.

Stress and your health

Every thought we have is translated through the brain to the nervous system and into the various systems of the body. For instance we blush when we are embarrassed, our heart will thump when we get a fright, we might want to urinate when we are nervous, and we may be overcome with nausea after witnessing an accident.

When the mind is relaxed and our thinking is positive, the body is free to function in a natural way and produces the necessary chemicals and energy to help us meet the challenges of the day.

However, when the mind is agitated or filled with fearful, angry or impatient thoughts the body reacts by releasing a cocktail of potent chemicals. These increase our alertness and arousal producing what is sometimes called an 'adrenalin buzz'. Although this response might help us survive in the middle of a war zone, it is not useful in the average work environment because our bodies simply can't sustain this level of stimulation. In the case of chronic stress, where a person 'runs on their nerves' the various systems eventually break down resulting in a range of health problems.

Franchisors and franchisees who work under continual pressure and stress need to be mindful that, unless they look after their physical, mental and emotional health needs, they may become susceptible to insomnia, panic attacks, high blood pressure, stroke and heart attack, fatigue, recurrent colds, allergies and rashes, migraines and headaches, digestive problems and back problems — just to name a few!

Don't get ICED

Burnout can result from a person feeling constant emotional, mental and physical exhaustion. The four main symptoms of serious burnout can be summed up in the acronym — **ICED** and result in the following symptoms:

Isolated — withdrawing and cutting off your communication with others, even with those who care most about you. Rather than spend time with colleagues, family or friends you prefer to sit alone 'veging out' in front of the television.

Cynical — doubting the motives of others, including the people you work with. For instance, you might find yourself dropping sarcastic remarks in meetings and losing interest in the wellbeing of others, even your customers.

Exhausted — lacking the physical, emotional and mental energy to face each day's challenges. You might have trouble getting up in the morning or spend an unusually long time vacillating over decisions.

Despondent — feeling emotionally low with loss of joy or enthusiasm for life. The future may seem unusually bleak. Whereas once you were surrounded by opportunities, now all you see is problems.

However, in most cases, rather than becoming totally burnt out, people under constant stress tend to show milder forms of the above symptoms.

The Three Bubbles of Coping

These stress related problems emerge because we have neglected to take the time to plan for a successful life as well as a successful business. Anyone wanting to commence a preventative program might find it useful to consider the following three areas of their life:
1. The outside world of work.
2. The interpersonal world of relationships.
3. The personal world of inner management.

I refer to these three areas as the 'Three Bubbles of Coping'.

Imagine that these three bubbles are floating on the sea of life, a sea which is full of turbulence and undercurrents. Pushing down on the bubbles are the pressures of daily living — not enough time, too much to do, strained relationships, unhappy customers, and so on.

Providing there is sufficient buoyancy to keep each of the bubbles floating we are able to hold up against these downward pressures. However the three bubbles are connected, so if we lose buoyancy in one area and it starts to go under, it can also pull down the other areas.

For instance as business pressures begin to get to us (work bubble) we go home feeling stressed and tired (personal bubble). When the children want attention we get irritated which creates tension and conflict in the home (relationship bubble).

It works in other ways too. If we haven't been caring for our health and become run down and out of shape it becomes more difficult to sustain high energy levels (personal bubble). As our inner enthusiasm slips so does our commitment to our business—and surprise, so do sales levels in the business (work bubble). With profits down we cancel the family holiday creating misery all around us (relationship bubble).

- **Cash flow pressures**
- **Too much/too little work**
- **Lack of resources**

- **Poor health**
- **Feeling stressed**
- **Self doubt**

- **Un-met expectations**
- **Interpersonal conflict**
- **Lack of support**

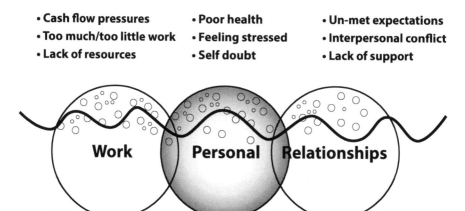

The Three Bubbles of Coping

The good news

The good news is that the process also works in reverse. If we have worked at building a strong, supportive family environment and good communication with our spouse or partner, this extra buoyancy in the relationship bubble can hold up the other bubbles when they come under pressure. For instance, when I came under significant work stress my wife's support was definitely a significant influence that helped me to get myself back on top of things.

Good health and a positive frame of mind is also incredibly helpful when dealing with work pressures or difficulties with relationships or family.

Similarly effective business management practices will reduce the risks of burnout. (A capable franchisor will have built many of these practices into the franchise system in the form of ongoing training and management reporting systems.) Being organised and having the right information at your fingertips is indeed a very powerful way of reducing stress. As one franchisee said to me:

"I made a loss in February, but I still happily went on holidays with my family in March because at least I had done my budgets and cash flows and knew exactly where I stood — I didn't have the fear of the unknown haunting me."

So focussing on building strong buoyancy in any one of the three bubbles of coping is a good start to preventing burnout. It is only when **all three areas** are weak that we start to sink.

Subtle Energy

I have used the word 'buoyancy' to describe the force that keeps the bubbles of life afloat. Probably a better word would be 'energy' because it is actually our level of energy or vitality that determines how well we cope with the things life throws at us.

Think about it. When you feel full of vitality and someone asks something of you, or something unexpected happens, how do you respond? Usually you may think, "Fine, no problem, I can handle that".

What if your energy is low? Your thinking is probably going to be more like, "Why can't they just go away and bother someone else!" or "Why me?"

Much of what happens in life is linked to energy issues. Yet energy is a mysterious force that is not very well understood.

In his book, *Subtle Energy*, Dr William Collinge says, "Real forces are moving within our bodies and the world around us — unseen, unheard, and some undetected by even the most sensitive scientific instruments. In recent years researchers have coined the term 'subtle energy' to describe these forces. While an understanding of subtle energies has been a part of many cultures and spiritual traditions for millennia, Western science is only now beginning to acknowledge they exist."

This subtle energy or life force not only influences our personal health and wellbeing, but also impacts on our relationships and our capacity to achieve what we want in life.

Be choosy with your friends

Because this is largely a book on relationships I want to say a few things specifically about the impact of relationships on health and wellbeing.

In Chapter 6, I pointed out that one of the four predictors of partnership breakdowns is the level and type of outside support the parties receive. In a marriage, friends or family can make or break a relationship through their comments and attitudes, while in a business partnership it may be your colleagues or professional advisers that influence your thinking in a positive or negative way.

An educator and yoga teacher, Vijay Yogendra, with whom I had the privilege of training for many years, used to say that if you go into a shed full of coal you will come out with some coal stuck to you; while if you go into a room full of fine gold particles some gold will stick to you. In other words, the people you associate with have a strong influence on how positive or negative you become.

You have probably had the experience of spending time with a positive person who is interested in you and relatively at peace with him or herself. When you leave their presence, you tend to feel good about yourself and life in general. Compare this to how you feel after you have spent time with someone who is negative and preoccupied with his or her own problems. It's a totally different experience because humans give out energy that can either be creative and healing, or destructive and draining. A doctor friend used to tell me that there were certain patients that, because they were so preoccupied with their own misery, would literally leave him feeling worn out. "It's as if they suck you dry and chew on your bones", he would say.

The message here is to be choosy about who you spend time with.

It's healthy to care

This relationship energy can have a significant positive impact on our health and wellbeing. For instance, in a major review of international studies on marriage, Dr Don Edgar, Ex-Director, Australian Institute of Family Studies, concluded, "What stands out from the research is that *quality of life is best predicted by one's relationship with a partner*".

Consider also the following research findings:

- An Ohio State University study found a correlation between whether women were happily married, and the functioning of their immune systems. They concluded that supportive relationships seem to act as a buffer against the damaging effects of stress on our health.

- A Stanford Medical School study found that women with advanced breast cancer who participated in a support group had *double* the survival time of those who did not.

- A study of ten thousand men that examined the relationship between marital happiness and heart disease found the most accurate predictor of angina was how they responded to the question, *"Does your wife show you her love?"*

- The incidence of heart attacks in an Italian community was half that of Americans with the same fat intake, smoking rates and cholesterol levels. The significant factor that distinguished the Italian group was that *they had unusually strong interpersonal relationships in their community.*

- A Harvard Medical School study found that when feelings of altruistic love and care were aroused in their subjects *their immune functioning was significantly boosted.*

- A recent study of 2,750 franchisees by our own team at the Franchise Relationships Institute examined the extent to which psychological and social factors could predict business performance. Of the sixteen factors that were examined, family and social support was one of the most significant predictors of success. For instance, franchisees who reported higher levels of family and social support were achieving 15% better financial performance.

So not only will positive relationships with others help you to run a more successful business, they will also help you to remain healthier and live longer.

Daily tips for your personal bubble

Of the three bubbles, the one that you have most control over is of course the personal bubble. So the rest of this chapter will mainly focus on this.

Here are some practical things you can do on a daily basis to build the energy in your personal bubble despite a busy or demanding lifestyle.

Relax

Regularly practise techniques that will help to slow a racing mind and promote mental calmness. These can include relaxation, meditation or, if you are religious, prayer. In the past people would absorb themselves in a creative hobby for relaxation but television has tended to put an end to this. There are many books, tapes and courses on the topic of relaxation and meditation. If you do attend a course, check the credentials of the teacher.

Wind down

Prepare yourself at the end of the day for a good night's sleep. Most people spend their day winding up their minds and then expect that they can turn their mind off at the end of the day like a computer. This seldom works because we lack training and self control over our thought processes.

Take time to wind down before going to bed. You might go for a walk, read the paper or sit quietly reflecting on the day. I have found that jotting down my thoughts in a diary can be a useful way of 'downloading' any unresolved worries or thoughts. I ask myself three questions:

* Do I have any outstanding worries or concerns from today?

* What might help to resolve this?

* Any final thoughts or reflections?

The final question provides me with an opportunity to write out and reinforce any specific attitudes that I have been practising such as being more patient, more positive, more tolerant of others, and so on.

Prioritise

Keep your priorities and values clear and spend time on the things that really matter. When there is so much to be done it's easy to get swept away by the apparent urgency of everything and lose sight of the important things — particularly health, family and peace of mind.

Concentrate

Bring a sense of concentration to your work. It's what you do in the present that counts, and will create your future results.

The past is history
The future is a mystery
Now is a gift
Which is why it is called 'the present'.

Incidentally, most of these tips will also help you with your golf game or your performance in any sport. The three things that sports psychologists train their athlete clients in are the abilities to maintain concentration, relaxation and a positive frame of mind under pressure.

Enjoy

Allow time each week to do the things you enjoy. Often we work hard and carry out our responsibilities to others but forget we also have a duty to ourselves. If you can bring that sense of relaxed concentration to your leisure, you will get even more value from it.

One of my neighbours loves beach fishing. As he describes what it's like standing on his favourite beach a big peaceful smile comes across his face. I'm sure this hobby contributes enormously to his health and wellbeing.

Believe

When facing difficulties maintain a belief in yourself, and in life, that things will work out for the best in the long run. Often we get down in the dumps because we assume things must happen in a particular way. It may be that a better opportunity is staring you in the face and you can't see it because of too narrow or short-term a perspective.

Accept

Accept the situations that life throws at you and deal with them in the best way you know how. I once read a beautiful saying in a book that went something like this:

"The secret to achieving balance and peace of mind is to accept that **What Is, Is, and What Isn't, Isn't**".

In other words, throwing a tantrum because things have turned out differently from what you wanted won't change a thing. No matter how strong your mind is you can't change what is.

Let go

Remove some of the emotional involvement from your work and just get on with doing what needs to be done. When we get angry we often read more into a situation than is really there. If a situation has upset you, try turning your attention to something completely different. Allow time for your emotions to settle down, then decide what should be done. Also remember that people don't make mistakes on purpose. Rather than wasting time and energy on blame, it's better to focus on what can be learned and what needs to be done to fix things.

Breathe

Our breathing is closely correlated to our vitality, our state of mind, the overall health of our nervous system and how long we live.

Observe how your breathing becomes shallow and irregular when you are anxious or angry compared with the deeper, slower breathing that occurs when you are relaxed or concentrated. This also works in reverse. Breathing deeply and evenly promotes a calmer, more focussed state of mind, which will improve your performance in stressful situations. The breath is also correlated with longevity — animals that breathe faster have shorter life spans and vice versa. Yet despite the importance of breathing to our health and wellbeing, most people have not been taught how to breathe properly.

Exercise

Take up a moderate but regular exercise routine that promotes good cardiovascular circulation (eg. walking) and the health of the nervous system. Stretching exercises like Yoga and Tai Chi, promote the health of the spinal column and optimise the free flow of nervous impulses from the brain to the various organs and systems of the body — thereby promoting good health and clear thinking.

Holidays

Holidays are another great way to boost your personal bubble. They also provide a valuable opportunity to 'hang out' with your family and rekindle the closeness that can be lost in the hurly burly of daily life.

Here are some thoughts on getting the most out of your well-earned breaks.

Decide what you want

Decide what you would like to get out of your holiday and choose a place that will meet this need. For example for family fun you will need activities that everyone enjoys, while if it is physical rejuvenation you are seeking then a health farm might be more suitable. A quiet spot by the sea or a place high up with expansive views would be ideal if you are looking for a fresh perspective.

Plug into nature

Holidays can rejuvenate us at the physical, mental and spiritual levels particularly if we choose a forest, mountain or seaside location. There is a powerful energy in nature that we can actually absorb if we take the time to appreciate it. A stroll through a forest or along a desolate beach, or just sitting in a quiet spot soaking in the beauty, will provide you with renewed feelings of vitality, clarity and joy. Some places have more natural energy than others so, if you find a spot that really works well for you, make it a regular visiting place.

Take a four by four

Several small breaks in a year are generally more effective than one long break. This works particularly well for people who find it difficult to leave their business for long periods. A particularly efficient approach is to take a four day break four times a year, including the weekend into the four days.

Prepare yourself

Ease into your holiday, rather than rushing off hassled and stressed. In the days before, talk with your family about how you would like the holiday to go and what you can each do to make it as pleasant as possible. Plan to allow yourself time to pack, organise the house, pets, and so on.

Tack onto a conference

If your franchise group holds regular conferences at pleasant locations, organise ahead to tack a few days onto the end. Use this time to reflect on the great ideas you have gained from the conference and how you will put them into practice. This provides you with a tax deductible excuse to invest in your wellbeing.

Sever your connections

While away sever all connections with your business. Leave the mobile and the lap top off and don't take calls unless there really is a genuine crisis. You can use the break as a test to see if you really are indispensable!

Leave performance pressure at the office

Balance your holiday with active and passive activities, but make sure they are all enjoyable. A competitive minded friend took his family to a beachside resort next to a beautiful national park. Rather than enjoy the slower pace with his family he felt driven to run ten kilometres by himself every day and subsequently damaged his leg sprinting up a mountain path. This ruined things for everyone.

Re-enter gently

Allow yourself a few hours to mentally prepare yourself for work. Once back in the business put your mind into what you are doing. While it is good to be grateful for the break you have had, if you try to hold onto your holiday feeling you'll just be disappointed.

Achieving greater life balance

There is a lot of discussion today on the concept of 'life balance'. While I have always been a great believer in the importance of life balance, I am sceptical when people talk about it as though it is something you achieve by rearranging your diary. Because someone decides to leave work at 5.30pm and spend every second Saturday watching their son play football, this does not mean they have achieved life balance.

Just spending more time with your family is not the key to achieving life balance. Life balance is not a time management issue. It is a mind management issue.

Being a balanced person has more to do with how you think, what motivates you and what your true values are than how you spend your time. In other words, it's about why you do the things you do. While this sounds simple it isn't, because human motivation is complex.

What's driving you?

Behind every action is a motive or intention. Motives tend to be subtle and difficult to read in others. We can also be unaware of our own motives. The extent to which we know and understand our motives is actually a good measure of our personal maturity and mental health.

Many people live a lifestyle of delusion because they do not understand what is really motivating or driving them. And so they get out of balance.

Below is a list of some basic human drives or motivations. You will see that each also has a 'dark side' or an unhealthy aspect which needs to be managed.

This dark side is more likely to become a problem if a person lacks maturity, insight, self discipline or has little sense of their own values. The result is they become driven by forces or compulsions that they do not understand. To me this is the real essence of being out of balance.

Some basic human motivations

Have a look at the following motivations. Which ones ring a bell for you?

MOTIVATION	BRIGHT SIDE	DARK SIDE
Achievement	To win and be the best	Perfectionistic, 'nothing is good enough', driven by a fear of failure
Affiliation	To get on with other people	Wanting to be liked by everyone; driven by the fear of rejection and avoiding conflict
Autonomy	To be independent and not have to rely on others	Self-centred, unable to collaborate with others, driven by a fear of losing control
Power	To be in a position of control	Dominating, aggressive, always protecting one's position, driven by a fear of being helpless
Security	To be prudent and careful	Overcautious, risk averse, driven by a fear of being uncomfortable
Service	To make a difference to the lives of others	Emotional burnout through over commitment, driven by a fear of not being needed
Status	To build reputation and gain public attention	Delusions of grandeur, believing one's own publicity, driven by a fear of inferiority
Knowledge	To be wise and have all the answers	Preoccupied with gathering information and being right; not asking for help when out of one's depth

When strengths become weaknesses

If you want to move toward a sense of balance in your work and your life you need to understand and manage the things that drive you. Some people call this 'personal mastery' and it is essential if you are serious about life balance.

As mentioned above this involves a combination of insight and discipline so you can understand and manage the positive and negative sides of your nature.

Our weaknesses are often our strengths taken to an extreme when we don't know when to stop. For instance, we can probably all relate to these everyday examples:

- A highly confident person can unintentionally intimidate others when they don't get their own way.

- A kind and sensitive person can become indecisive when tough decisions are needed.

- A creative person can create chaos around them if they keep reinventing the wheel.

- A well-organised person can become rigid and counter productive if they are not prepared to change their plans when necessary.

Incorporating positive values

In addition to the inner drives that motivate us, our values have a powerful influence over our lives and our sense of balance.

What we value and believe shapes our relationship with the world, how we spend our time, how we evaluate our experiences, and ultimately, impacts on our ability to function effectively. Good values help us to modify our behaviour in a more positive direction, especially when we feel the urge to go with our compulsions.

Our values also influence our self-esteem because they help us to define who we are. Surely this is what balance is all about — who you are — not what you have done.

Some values that help to build inner confidence and balance include:

- Doing things because you believe they need to be done rather than because you feel compelled to do them. This sometimes means being tough and uncompromising on the things that matter, despite inconvenience or resistance from others.

- Being tolerant and open minded when dealing with others, especially when they see things differently to you. It is easy to be closed minded and judgemental but it takes courage to see things from someone else's point of view.

- Trying to be helpful and of service, even when you get no feedback or recognition for this. You don't have to be a philanthropist. While it's good to put something back into the community that has enabled you to become successful, small acts of kindness practised consistently with the people you deal with on a daily basis are often more important. Ironically, we often have the biggest influence on others' lives when we are not trying to do so.

- Being grateful for life and the opportunity to live, learn and have all sorts of interesting experiences. This is also a powerful value, almost like a medicine, because it prevents us from succumbing to feelings of being a victim when we don't immediately get our own way.

Smiling and crying

A saintly man was once wandering through a village when he heard a lot of noise and joyful music coming from one of the homes. Upon entering he asked what all the fuss was about.

"Oh, we are all so very happy", someone shouted. "We have just had a little baby born into our village."

The saint replied, "Could I ask for some silence please". Everyone fell silent, except of course for the sound of the baby, who was crying its heart out.

"You see what's happening here. Here is a baby that has just been born and it is crying while all of you smile", he remarked.

"I recommend that you live your life in such a fashion that the day you go, you are smiling while everybody is crying."

The balanced individual

One final word on this topic of balance.

Like all the worthwhile things in life — positive relationships, good health, peace of mind — balance is a process, not a destination. We are always moving toward equilibrium and often, just as we think we have found it, things change and more work is needed.

People I know who I regard as being more balanced human beings tend to respond in a relaxed and natural manner to the needs of the situations in which they find themselves. They do not achieve balance by dividing their days into neat segments of work, family, social activity, sport and so on. Rather they treat all their activities as an opportunity to contribute, to grow and to do what is needed in order to achieve their goals and be true to their values.

So next time you consider the question of whether your life is in balance, rather than just looking at what you are doing, you may find it more useful to consider why you are doing it.

In the final analysis it is the balance in your thinking rather than the balance in your diary that counts.

Where to start

What we have covered in this chapter is an overall commitment to self-improvement. If you are not sure where to start try completing the following sentence.

"What tends to get me into trouble is ......". Chances are you have just identified the most important area you need to work on right now. And chances are your efforts will bring greater success to you and your business.

To finish this chapter I would like to share a beautiful little poem on success by philosopher, Ralph Waldo Emerson.

How do you measure success?

To laugh often and much,
To win the respect of intelligent people,
And the affection of children.

To earn the appreciation of honest critics,
And to endure the betrayal of false friends.

To appreciate beauty,
To find the best in others,
To leave the world a bit better,
whether by a healthy child, a garden patch,
a redeemed social condition, or a job well done.

To know even one other life has breathed easier,
because you have lived.

THIS, is to have succeeded.

In summary

Franchisees and franchisor executives face considerable pressure in their day to day work. Poorly managed stress increases the chances of business failure, health problems and burnout. By investing the time and energy to build a successful life as well as a successful business you will enjoy greater freedom, satisfaction and enjoyment.

Action Tips:

- Review how you are coping in the three bubbles of life. Is there enough buoyancy in your bubbles?

- Pick one bubble and draw up an action plan of what you will do to get this aspect of your life into better shape.

- Choose your friends carefully and consciously spend time with like-minded people who are supportive of your goals. Never underestimate the positive power of good relationships.

- Take up a moderate exercise routine and a relaxation technique and practise them every day.

- Prepare yourself for a good night's sleep.

- Put a priority on spending time on the things that really matter — health, family and peace of mind — or you won't fit them in.

- Maintain a belief in yourself and in life that things will work out for the best in the long run.

- Plan to take several short holidays each year.

- Make a commitment to get to know yourself. Complete the sentence "What tends to get me into trouble is ..." and set yourself a lifetime goal to take charge of your mind and your life rather than letting your mind and compulsions drive you.

- Embrace values that will contribute to your personal pride and peace of mind and use these to guide your behaviour, particularly during times of hardship.

CHAPTER FIFTEEN
What the Mind Conceives the Mind Achieves

The last chapter explored the topic of stress and life balance. In this chapter we will examine how you can use the power of your mind to create the business and the life that you want.

Why me?

Have you ever found yourself in a situation where despite your hard work and commitment, you find yourself making little headway?

Perhaps your colleagues or staff are not accepting your ideas, your customers are unappreciative of your sacrifices or you have not been able to achieve the results you anticipated. What happens in these situations is we become increasingly frustrated and cynical and can find ourselves joining the passing parade of life's victims — head down, mumbling and cursing "Why me?"

Of course if we stepped back and looked at our situation more objectively we could just as easily ask "Why not me?" After all it is I who chose to take on this project, start this business, join this organisation, marry this person, or whatever it is that's been troubling us.

The fact is that most problems we face in life are largely of our own choosing.

Where preparation meets opportunity

In Chapter thirteen I wrote about the characteristics of people who cope well with challenge and change. (See page 139 — "Are you a hardy or a softy?") One of these is an 'internal locus of control' or a belief that we have a large degree of control over what happens to us in life. If we want to live a happy and successful life we simply have no choice but to embrace this fundamental truth.

Of course there will always be things that occur outside of our control. For instance, while we might be able to *influence* other people's thinking, we can't *control* their behaviour. And destiny, luck, providence or whatever you want to call it will always throw situations or challenges in our way. But it is up to us how we respond. We can choose to drop our bundle and sit in a corner like a victim or we can summon the courage to look around and seek out the opportunities that are also waiting for our attention.

Successful entrepreneurs intuitively understand this. Their minds are like the automatic seek button on your car radio. When things go off track or get fuzzy, rather than cursing the static, they simply set about tuning into new opportunities.

The other day I heard it put another way. I was flying back from a conference listening to an interview between Oprah Winfrey and Julia Roberts who was explaining that her fame was due to a lucky break. Oprah made the interesting comment that she believed that what people call luck is "where preparation meets opportunity."

Thousands of decisions

Every day each of us is faced with thousands of opportunities to do virtually whatever we like. Even in situations where we might think there is no choice we can still talk to whomever we like, focus our attention wherever we like and think whatever we like.

The situations we find ourselves in — good, bad or indifferent — are the result of many large and small decisions that we have made. Bit by bit, each decision has guided us to our present predicament. It is a continuous, almost invisible process that has brought us into the present and will create our future, depending on what we decide to do next.

Even when we fail to make a decision, for instance through fear or lack of confidence, we are making a decision — we choose not to choose. And we cannot but face the consequences of this decision. Our work or our debts pile up, communication with others deteriorates, and possibly worst of all, we lose motivation. When asked about the secret to his incredible work output, Leonardo De Vinci is said to have made the comment "Inaction saps the vitality of the mind".

The book that you are reading didn't just appear in your hand. You decided to pick it up. Prior to that you decided to purchase it, borrow it or accept it as a gift. This book is in your hands because of hundreds, maybe thousands, of small decisions that you have made.

And here's a more profound idea. There is a reason why you are reading it. (I presume that no-one is forcing you!)

Turning obstacles into stepping stones

You might be interested to know that before completing this book, I had several business set backs. In the space of five weeks three significant projects I had been working on for a year or more simply fell to pieces.

After initially feeling sorry for myself and contemplating the unfairness of what had happened, I saw the situation from a different perspective.

I realised that although these projects had not turned out the way I had hoped it had been my decision to take them on because I had been confident they would succeed. In hindsight there were a number of factors working against me, some under my control and many beyond my control. The real question I needed to ask was not "Why me?" or even "What went wrong?" It was "What now?"

This insight was important because it gave me back my sense of control. I reminded myself that it is my life and that each decision I make will determine what happens next.

So I decided to spend the extra time I had on my hands turning the concept for this book into a finished product. I guess we can both thank my business disasters for this!

Some people call this process of shifting our thinking from victim to active participant, turning obstacles into stepping stones.

The self fulfilling prophesy

One of the earliest popular books on how our thinking influences our behaviour is *Psycho-Cybernetics* by Dr Maxwell Maltz. Although written in the 1950's I still regard it as one of the best books available today on how the unconscious mind shapes and guides our lives.

Maltz likened the human mind to the cybernetic guiding system in a rocket. Once a target has been set for the rocket, its cybernetic system constantly adjusts its course through thousands of small decisions, keeping it moving toward its goal.

Humans, he believed, also have targets in the form of their goals, their beliefs and their expectations. Our mind guides us toward these targets through the many decisions and actions we take each day.

In Chapter five I suggested that our expectations of other people can significantly change their behaviour through the 'Pygmalion Effect'. This principle also applies to ourselves. Our self expectation influences what we focus on and how we use our energy, which of course determines what we ultimately achieve. Henry Ford's famous quote, "Whether you think you can or you think you can't — you're right both ways", is very apt.

In his excellent book, *Yes You Can*, goal setting expert, Jack Collis, expresses the self fulfilling prophesy this way:

"Vividly imagined events, supported by purposeful action and sustained by faith and belief, come to pass."

This leads us to the important concept of goal setting.

The power of written goals

Bill McGowan, Founder of Fastway Couriers, is a fanatical goal setter, and attributes his substantial business success to this habit. What is also interesting about Bill is the story of how he discovered the power of writing down and reviewing his goals. Here it is in his words.

"I used to be an angry young man. If someone disagreed with me I would just thump them. But I wasn't happy with this approach to dealing with my frustration and knew that I needed a way to channel my energy in a more positive direction.

"One day one of my University lecturers gave a small session on goal setting. After the lecture I chased him back to his room and asked him if he could show me more. He said that he didn't actually practise goal setting himself but he told me a bit more about the theory and referred me to a few books.

"From that time I have written down goals in all areas of my life. Every day I review and update my goals. I carry them around with me in my Goal Book at all times.

"Instead of taking my aggression out on other people I now use my aggression to make me set goals and because I set goals I am motivated to achieve them. I give myself a good kick up the backside to make me do it.

"So I have found my answer on how to manage my aggression and make money at the same time. Goal setting in the written form is hard work and uses up all that aggression."

What is fascinating about Bill's story is that no one else in his class chose to accept the advice that the lecturer had offered them. Even the lecturer himself chose not to use his own information!

But Bill had prepared his mind. He was looking for a way to use his energy creatively and he found it. It wasn't luck. He was there waiting at the crossroads where preparation meets opportunity.

What is also inspiring about Bill's story is that he consciously took a part of his personality that could have potentially created big problems for himself and used this purposely to achieve something meaningful in his life.

The laughing doctor

Toward the end of my formal psychology training I had the privilege of spending a few weeks with Dr Hiroki Takashima, an international author and psychiatrist. Dr Takashima was an expert in Logotherapy, which emphasises the importance of meaning and purpose to psychological and spiritual health.

Despite his 65 years of age, only having one lung and suffering from a chronic vertigo condition, Dr Takashima was a vibrant man who brought humour and purpose to every situation he found himself in. He would challenge and provoke his patients to think about why they thought the things they thought and did the things they did. He would make them laugh and open their minds to new, creative ways of looking at their problems. And although he was provocative he always treated people with the utmost sensitivity and respect.

The power of purpose

Logotherapy was originally developed by Victor Franki, a psychiatrist and World War 2 holocaust survivor, who lived through the most terrifying experiences. While going through this living hell Franki realised that human beings are fundamentally meaning seeking creatures who must have purpose in their lives if they are to be well and happy. He noticed that the people in the Concentration Camps who survived, including himself, were those who maintained a faith or a belief that their suffering had a purpose. For instance, that they would eventually be reunited with their families, or that they would not allow the Nazis to take away their dignity. He observed that many of those who died were people who could find no meaning in their suffering and therefore gave up hope. Victor Franki's ideas and experiences are recorded in his fascinating book, *Man's Search for Meaning*.

Even somewhere as horrific as a concentration camp, it is possible to maintain one's sense of choice and self-determination.

How thinking rules behaviour

These two principles, the power of choice and the power of purpose, permeate our lives. What happens on the outside is a reflection of processes going on inside us. Simply put, our thinking guides our behaviour. Our values, beliefs and expectations inevitably dictate what we will avoid, what we will try and when and if we will give up.

Sometimes the process is conscious. For instance, when we set specific goals or have a clear vision in our mind as to how we want things to turn out.

However, subconsciously, this process is also happening all the time. Our thinking dictates our priorities, how we spend our time and the hundreds of small, yet significant decisions we make every hour.

This explains why people end up doing the things they do: why some people seem to have one lucky break after another while others face one crisis after another; why some people divorce one person and then marry someone almost identical in looks and personality. It's not coincidence — it's a choice.

So we can either choose to set our own goals or have our subconscious mind do it for us. The problem with leaving it to the subconscious is that, for most people, the subconscious mind is full of fears and desires that, if allowed to take charge, are going to lead them down a path of misery and distraction.

So just making decisions based on how you feel is not a great idea, unless you have a very disciplined mind and a lot of self awareness. I don't know about you but I would much rather take control of my mind and my life, than just drift down an unknown path to an unknown destination.

Selecting staff

We have all come across businesses which have a natural vitality and where we experience a genuine attitude of care. Where staff members are exceptionally pleasant and our needs are met quickly, efficiently and without fuss. Is this just good management or is something else at work here?

If we were to ask the owner of such a business how she manages to find such great staff she might say, "I have always been lucky with my staff." But we know that luck is where 'preparation meets opportunity'. Her luck has been created by her own mind because she has been carrying a vision around in her mind of the way that her staff should feel, look and behave when dealing with customers.

She will have consciously or subconsciously rejected people that have not fitted her vision while behaving favourably toward people that do. She will have reinforced the attitudes and values that she wants her staff to embrace. And she will have harnessed the power of the Pygmalion Effect. Her inner vision has ultimately been projected into her business through her thinking and her behaviour.

What's your vision?

In so many areas, without even trying, we all have enormous power and control over what is happening to us and around us.

Think about the sort of environment you want to create in your business. How would you like your staff to behave? What sort of relationship do you want to have with your franchisor or franchisees? What sort of experience would you like your customers to have?

The next question is whether you are prepared to do whatever it takes to achieve this. If so, you will attract the people that will help you make this happen. But you must have faith.

The clearer you are about what you want, the more you can consciously guide this process. The process of goal setting is one way of harnessing the power of your mind and putting it to good use.

'Future Search' goal setting exercise

Here is a simple process that you can complete alone or with a group to help you develop a vision or some key goals for your business. It is based on a process called 'Future Search.'

Step 1 — List your goals

Write down what you would personally like to see happening in 1 to 2 years time in your business if you and the people in your business are as effective as might reasonably be expected. What visible and tangible results would you like to see as a result of your terrific work?

Create a list of desired outcomes or goals, for instance:
- Our administrative systems are fully integrated.
- The business is achieving 15% EBITO.
- I am spending at least one full day a week with my family.
- We have expanded into China.
- The business is no longer dependent on my daily involvement.

Step 2 — Define your stakeholders

Make a list of all the people with a stake in your business, ie. they are affected for better or worse by what happens. This could include:

- People on whom you depend for knowledge or resources, eg. your franchisor, franchisees, consultants, suppliers

- Customers

- Staff

- Families of customers and staff

- Competitors

Taking into account these 'stakeholders', consider if any goals should be added to your list from Step 1.

Step 3 — Define constraints

Make a list of any things that might limit or constrain you in working toward your goals. For instance:

- Restrictions your stakeholders might put on you, eg. you may only be able to sell certain types of products

- Financial restrictions

- Government restrictions

- A shortage of qualified staff

Consider if any of the goals from your list should be changed by these limitations.

Step 4 — Define final list of goals

Pick the top 10 goals that are most appealing and meaningful to you. You may want to rewrite these using the SMART formula, ie:

- Make them as **Specific** as possible

- Make them **Measurable** so you will know when they have been achieved

- Ensure that the people responsible for carrying out the actions **Agree** to do this

- Make sure the goal is **Realistic** given the current circumstances

- Make sure it is **Time bound** to a finishing date

For instance, taking some of the outcomes from the examples in Step 1, they could be expressed as follows:

- By December 2017 all our administrative systems will be linked to the one software platform.
- By June 2018 the business will be running efficiently without my direct day-to-day involvement.
- By 2019 we will have 700 stores in China.

Now you would need to develop a specific list of tasks to turn this goal into reality.

Ultimately we get the staff, the customers, the suppliers and the franchisor or franchisees that we deserve. It's a case of 'What the mind conceives the mind achieves'.

In summary

All human beings are continuously moving toward the goals that they set themselves — either consciously or unconsciously. People who have clear long-term goals and who ensure these goals are consistent with their values have more meaning in their lives and are more psychologically healthy. Goal setting enables you to capture the things that are important to you and put a framework around them. By writing down your goals you increase their potency and make them more likely to come true.

Action Tips:

- Whenever you feel like a victim, remind yourself that it's your life and you make all the choices.
- Write down your goals, review them every day, support them with purposeful action and maintain a belief that they will come to pass.
- Fill your life with purposeful and meaningful work. You'll be healthier and happier as a result.
- Create a detailed vision for your business by imagining the future as it would be if you and the people in your business had worked as effectively as possible. Write out the results of your imagined future and turn these into goals.

CHAPTER SIXTEEN

Developing High Performance Franchisees

While franchising is a partnership between franchisees and franchisor, franchisees ultimately hold the key to the success of a franchise system. After all it is their performance that drives sales, enhances customer satisfaction, creates brand loyalty and delivers the franchisor its royalties.

Being able to assess the suitability and ongoing performance of franchisees is thus critical to the long-term success of any franchise system. This chapter will look at how to prevent weak links in your franchise chain. It includes an instrument you can use to assess the competence and learning needs of franchisees in your system, or apply to yourself.

The rule of thirds

When I ask franchisors about the calibre and performance of their franchisees I am typically told that a third are 'great', a third are 'okay' and a third 'need work'. In other words they follow a normal distribution (see graph opposite).

The challenge for franchisors is to constantly move their existing franchisees to the right to create a 'skewed' distribution; in other words to continually 'raise the bar'. With regard to franchisee selection the challenge is to screen out people who are likely to 'need work' and attract and select those who will be 'great'. (See diagram on page 170.)

Why franchisees go off the rails

To raise the competence of franchisees is easier said than done because people are complex and there are many factors that contribute to, or detract from, franchisee performance. Also a potential franchisee who initially appears to be highly suitable may turn out unsuitable for a number of reasons which go beyond their bank balance or personality style.

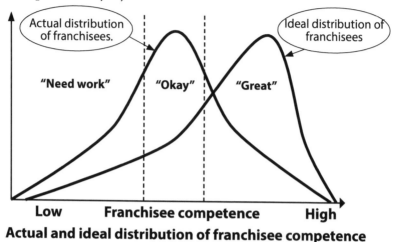

Actual and ideal distribution of franchisee competence

Take the following common examples:

- Subtle but important information may have been skillfully hidden from the franchisor by a potential franchisee that is overly keen to take on a franchise opportunity. For instance the person may not have disclosed a health problem that later interferes with their ability to run the business.

- Life events or significant family changes may significantly alter a franchisee's outlook or their approach to running their business. For instance acrimonious family breakups can send a business off the rails.

- Business circumstances outside the franchisor or franchisee's control may significantly or fundamentally change the nature of the business, turning a normally positive and flexible person into a disappointed cynic. A previously good site may, for instance, become unviable due to changes in parking or local shopping habits.

- Rapid and continuous business growth may challenge a franchisee beyond their competence level and lead to poor performance or burn out. A franchisee couple who ran an excellent business may be unable to cope as they start to employ outside staff.

- An issue of significance in a franchisee's mind may have been badly handled by the franchisor thus undermining the franchisee's confidence and willingness to work cooperatively with the franchisor.

- Even the most successful franchisees can suffer from 'rust out' after they have been in the system for a long time. While their business may have been profitable for some time, they may start to lose interest, let things slip and become difficult to deal with.

The RACE to success

As we saw in Chapter 2 successful franchisees do three things well:

- They run a profitable business.
- They grow a base of happy customers.
- They support the values of the franchise organisation and brand (eg. quality, service, reliability, or whatever it is that your competitive edge is based on).

In other words, they are people who will grow their business 'in sync' with the culture and philosophy of the franchisor.

To deliver on these areas franchisees need a balance of strengths, what I call 'attributes for success'. (Human Resource people call these competencies.) These can be skills, knowledge, values, drives or other characteristics. They also need to have a minimum of attributes that are likely to undermine their success. I call these 'negative omens'.

Research by our team of psychologists at the Franchise Relationships Institute has shown there are between 20 and 28 attributes for success depending on the franchise system. These fall into four broad areas:

Relationship skills are needed to create loyalty and trust from customers and staff. We all know that successful businesses are built on happy, loyal customers and enthusiastic, hard working staff.

Analytical and financial skills are needed to regularly review business performance. Franchisees must be able to monitor key performance indicators if their business is to remain on track.

Commitment and stamina are needed to manage the demands of the business. For instance, franchisees need to be robust and capable of grinding out the long hours and often repetitive work, without letting their standards slip.

Entrepreneurial drive is needed to spot opportunities to develop the business. Franchisees need to constantly seek out new opportunities for growth in their local markets while not letting the competition get them down.

If a franchisee is weak in one or more of these areas their business will probably falter and possibly fail. Over the years, through case studies and ongoing research, I have collected a list of the attributes that are associated with troublesome franchisees, poorly performing franchisees or franchisees that have gone broke even though their business was potentially sound. You will find some of these 'negative omens' at www.franchiserelationships.com in the Franchisee Suitability section.

High Performance Franchising Indicator

Are you 'franchisee of the year' material?

Some time ago I was asked to develop a list of detailed criteria for judging a National Franchisee of the Year Award. Many franchisees from a wide range of different businesses who entered the Awards reported that they gained enormous benefit from going through the process of reviewing themselves and their operations against these criteria. I have thus provided a High Performance Franchising Indicator on pages 174-175, which enables you to assess yourself or a franchisee on eleven attributes for success and pinpoint specific learning and development needs. (This is a shortened version of a more comprehensive management tool we have developed for the franchising sector.)

How to complete the Indicator

Decide who you are going to rate and put yourself in an objective frame of mind. If you are rating yourself you might like to use someone as a 'reality check'. Read each performance indicator, decide how fully it describes the behaviour of the franchisee (or yourself) and circle the relevant response. Note that most of the indicators are very specific so you should only circle 3 if it fully and accurately describes what this person does. If they have partly done this you should circle 2. If they have not done this at all you should circle 1. Then total the points. You should end up with a score between 33 and 99.

Interpreting Scores

83 and above — Excellent. According to your assessment this person is definitely in the High Performance range. They should be encouraged to take on additional challenges within the franchise system such as a bigger business, a role on the Franchise Advisory Council, etc.

70 to 82 — Good. According to your assessment this person is a competent franchisee. However there are areas (rated 2 or 1) where they may benefit from training and development. Consider which of these will create the most immediate benefit and develop an action plan.

60 to 69 — Weak. According to your assessment there are many areas where this person could improve their performance. A detailed review with ongoing follow up would be beneficial.

Less than 60 — Poor. According to your assessment this person has many weaknesses that will need to be addressed if they are to have a future in franchising. A serious review would be in order.

In summary

The long-term success of a franchise system depends almost entirely on the suitability and ongoing performance of its franchisees. Franchisors should therefore select their franchisees carefully. Raising the competence of existing franchisees is also not that easy because there are many factors that contribute to running a successful franchise and some of these cannot be easily learned.

Action Tips:

- Create a thorough franchisee selection system with checklists so that important information is not accidentally missed during the selection process.

- Develop a profile of your ideal franchisee and a rating system whereby candidates can be assessed against this profile.

- Use professional selection tools such as behavioural interviewing and profiling to assist you in understanding the strengths and weaknesses of potential franchisees.

- Put your existing franchisees (or yourself) through the High Performance Franchising Indicator over the page to determine learning and development needs.

- Create new challenges for high performance franchisees so their energy and talent is properly utilised.

High Performance Franchising Indicator

Person being rated: _____

Name of rater: _____

Uses business planning processes	Yes	Partly	No
1. Has, in last 12 months, conducted a formal analysis of the local market looking at trends, threats and opportunities	3	2	1
2. Has a current list of specific business goals with measurable outcomes (eg sales, profit, customer growth)	3	2	1
3. Reviews the business's actual performance against goals or performance indicators at least every three months	3	2	1
Keeps accurate financial records			
4. Has developed a detailed annual income and expenses budget	3	2	1
5. Monitors the business's cash flow and liquidity position at least fortnightly	3	2	1
6. Prepares monthly profit statements and checks these against the budget	3	2	1
Family is supportive of the business			
7. Family members talk about the business in positive terms	3	2	1
8. Family members are happy to help out in the business when needed	3	2	1
9. Stable and positive family environment— no major crises	3	2	1
Keeps organised and maintains high standards			
10. Plans daily work activities according to a regular system (eg diary or business planner)	3	2	1
11. Office or van and customer contact points always clean and professionally presented	3	2	1
12. Has checklists and systems to manage every aspect of the business	3	3	1
Maintains high levels of health and wellbeing			
13. Does at least 20 minutes exercise every day and follows a sensible health regime (eg a reasonable diet)	3	2	1
14. Keeps the pressures of the business in perspective— doesn't lose their cool under stress	3	2	1
15. Has sensibly addressed any outstanding health problems (eg visited a doctor for a check up)	3	2	1

Generates a motivating team environment for staff	Yes	Partly	No
16. Articulates an exciting vision for the business and encourages staff to embrace this	3	2	1
17. Provides all staff with access to quarterly personal development activities (eg courses, team building)	3	2	1
18. Has ongoing incentives for staff and ensures they all receive regular positive feedback	3	2	1
Actively participates in the franchise program			
19. Networks with and shares information with other franchisees at least monthly	3	2	1
20. Positively participates in all franchise meetings	3	2	1
21. Supports and promotes the values of the franchise system	3	2	1
Effectively resolves differences with others			
22. Raises issues of concern directly with the people who can do something about it	3	2	1
23. Maintains good relationships with all business stakeholders (eg. staff, suppliers, franchisor, franchisees)	3	2	1
24. Resolves conflicts diplomatically so that long term relationships with others are preserved	3	2	1
Relates well with customers			
25. Is outgoing, optimistic and upbeat; uses positive language when interacting with others	3	2	1
26. Builds rapport and empathy with other people; has a reputation as a great person to deal with	3	2	1
27. New customers regularly come through word of mouth	3	2	1
Promotes the business in the local market			
28. Regularly runs promotional programs in cooperation with other local businesses	3	2	1
29. Has an up to date database of customers and makes some type of personalised contact at least twice a year	3	2	1
30. Has a promotional calender of forthcoming local marketing activities tied to a budget	3	2	1
Maintains an openness to learning and change			
31. Maintains a monthly self improvement plan (eg. reads a book or attends a course every month	3	2	1
32. Welcomes feedback from others on their strengths and weaknesses (eg. from staff, franchisor or customers)	3	2	1
33. Accepts change as one of the necessary costs of keeping up with the market	3	2	1
TOTAL SCORE			

See pages 172-173 for interpretation of Total Score

CHAPTER SEVENTEEN

How You Can Achieve a Profitable Partnership

In this final chapter we will review some practical approaches that franchisors and franchisees can take to maintain profitable partnerships with each other.

Measuring franchisee satisfaction

"If you can't measure it you can't manage it" — so the saying goes. However while the financial aspects of a business are typically measured on an ongoing basis, 'people issues' such as morale and satisfaction are seldom measured, not because they are unimportant, but because it is regarded as too hard to do.

The fact is that you *can* measure attitudes and feelings. For instance I have developed a franchisee satisfaction survey that franchisors can use to better understand what, specifically, they can do to improve their franchisee's level of satisfaction.

The benefits of such surveys are that they can provide valuable information on how a franchisor can deliver the best value possible to its franchisees. In particular information can be gained on the following areas.

The usefulness of specific services — services that are costly to provide may be regarded by franchisees as not useful. Knowing this, the franchisor can redistribute its limited resources to better meet the needs of its franchisees.

Commitment to specific initiatives — this is especially important during times of change. If franchisees do not have a commitment or belief in the strategies of the franchisor these are bound to fail.

Perception of franchisor staff — the best way to find out how to improve your level of service to someone is to ask them. Surveys that ask franchisees to rate franchisor staff on specific behaviours can provide powerful feedback for improving communication.

Franchisee satisfaction — issues to do with franchisee satisfaction are really measuring people's perceptions rather than objective reality. However, it is again worth remembering that 'when perception meets reality, reality comes out second best'.

I recommend that a comprehensive survey be conducted at least every two years.

Some of the things I suggest you look at when measuring franchisee satisfaction include the following.

- The confidence that franchisees have in the leadership being shown by the franchisor.

- How satisfied franchisees are with the practical and moral support they are receiving.

- The extent to which franchisees feel a sense of pride and belonging to the group.

- Whether franchisees feel they have ready access to the information they need.

- The extent to which franchise meetings are seen as useful and frequent enough.

- The extent to which franchisees feel in conflict with their franchisor.

- The extent to which franchisees feel their financial expectations and personal aspirations are being fulfilled.

- How confident franchisees feel about the future of their business.

- Whether continuous improvement and innovation are seen to be encouraged.

- Whether franchisees feel performance and achievement are adequately recognised.

- How interesting and enjoyable they find their work.

- How stressful they find their work.

What franchisees want

One question I like to ask franchisees is who specifically in their franchisor company do they admire and respect the most. The people who are mentioned tend to come from a range of sitions — General Managers, Accounts Clerks, Field Advisers or Receptionists.

When I ask them *why* they picked these people, the following six attributes are consistently mentioned. So if you work for a franchisor and want to gain the respect and cooperation of your franchisees, practice these behaviours more consistently.

1. Listen attentively

Make an attempt to understand the franchisee's needs and ideas. Even if you don't agree, rather than being defensive or fobbing them off, you can still communicate your understanding of their point of view.

2. Get things done

Be reliable and follow through on your commitments. If you say you will call back on Monday, call back on Monday. If you say you will be out to visit on Tuesday at 3.30pm, arrive on time — no excuses.

3. Show concern

Be genuinely helpful and interested in your franchisees' success. For instance, when talking with them ask how things are going. If you believe that they need something that will help them to achieve their goals, try to find a way to get it for them.

4. Communicate directly

Be straightforward, direct and open in your dealings. Don't beat around the bush — say what you mean and mean what you say. If an issue has been discussed make sure there is clarity on what has been agreed.

5. Be technically competent

Make sure you have the knowledge and skills to handle franchisee enquiries and provide them with effective support. If you need extra development in an area then get it. And if you don't know something, say so and find out.

6. Maintain a positive approach

No matter how much a franchisee may complain, they in fact want you to maintain a positive approach. So don't indulge in gossip about other people or give the impression that you have lost confidence in the franchise system. Focus on what needs to be done to fix problems rather than dwelling on the problems themselves or who is to blame.

Keeping the CEO's finger on the pulse

If I had a criticism of many franchisor Chief Executive Officers it would be that they become too far removed from their franchisees. Maintaining a focus on long-term strategic issues is no excuse for losing touch with the day to day concerns of franchisees, who are the real lifeblood of the franchise system.

At their best, franchise networks function like communities where franchisee members feel a strong sense of belonging and commitment to the group. Such commitment is only possible where the CEO stays close to the hearts and minds of his or her franchisees.

A process that can achieve this in an efficient and effective manner is for the CEO to conduct regular 'rap' sessions or focus groups with small groups of franchisees. These can run for up to two hours and address whatever franchisees want to talk about. The CEO may also want to use this more intimate setting to bounce some thoughts off the franchisees. These groups can be run close to the franchisees' premises in a pleasant and quiet setting such as a private hotel or coffee lounge.

Franchisors and franchisees who regularly participate in these groups claim they not only enjoy them, but that they improve mutual understanding of operational and strategic issues.

Franchisors who regularly keep in touch with the experience, hopes and concerns of their franchisees in this way are collecting valuable information on how the organisation is performing as a service provider. They are also demonstrating practical concern for the opinions of their franchisees and the company's commitment to continuous improvement.

A checklist for franchisors

If you work for a franchisor company there is a checklist on page 180 which you can complete by ticking the box that best describes your company's approach. Be objective and base your rating on facts, not wishful thinking. This is a useful exercise for a franchisor management team to complete together.

Poor performance in any one of these areas can cause disputes between franchisees and franchisors. In other words, a franchisor who puts a 'seldom' or 'never' next to one or more of these statements would be well advised to review its *modus operandi*.

Franchisor Relationship Checklist

		Tick One:	Never	Seldom	Often	Always
1.	We promptly inform our franchisees of new developments.		☐	☐	☐	☐
2.	We hold regular face to face meetings with our franchisees.		☐	☐	☐	☐
3.	We involve some franchisees in the planning and running of these meetings.		☐	☐	☐	☐
4.	We have formal channels for franchisees to put forward ideas to improve the franchise concept.		☐	☐	☐	☐
5.	We reward the efforts and outstanding performance of our franchisees.		☐	☐	☐	☐
6.	Franchisees can depend on us because we deliver on our promises.		☐	☐	☐	☐
7.	We consult with franchisees on significant issues that will affect them before making final decisions.		☐	☐	☐	☐
8.	Our field advisers have the skills to help franchisees improve their sales and profitability.		☐	☐	☐	☐
9.	We monitor the profitability of franchisees and step in if we see a problem.		☐	☐	☐	☐
10.	We monitor the development of each franchisee and try to determine their needs at different stages.		☐	☐	☐	☐
11.	We innovate and keep our system and our image up-to-date with changing market trends.		☐	☐	☐	☐
12.	We have organised advantageous purchasing arrangements for our franchisees.		☐	☐	☐	☐
13.	We treat our franchisees with the respect of business partners — not like employees.		☐	☐	☐	☐
14.	We fulfil our contractual obligations to our franchisees.		☐	☐	☐	☐
15.	If we make a mistake we don't try to cover it up or shift the blame—we give the facts and fix the problem.		☐	☐	☐	☐
16.	If there is a conflict we address it promptly in a conciliatory spirit.		☐	☐	☐	☐
17.	We have a clear vision of our network's values, mission and goals, which we communicate to franchisees at every opportunity.		☐	☐	☐	☐

The seven deadly sins of franchisees

Although franchisors have a responsibility to effectively manage the franchise relationship, franchisees also must take responsibility for keeping their franchisor on side.

If you are a franchisee here are seven types of behaviour guaranteed to get your franchisor offside. Perhaps we could call them the seven deadly sins of franchisees.

1. Playing the Blame Game

I have pointed out in several places throughout this book that human beings have an uncanny ability to interpret events to suit their own interests. For instance, when sales are going well franchisees often attribute this to their own hard work and talent. But if sales drop franchisors are often blamed, sometimes unfairly, which only frustrates and de-motivates them.

Instead of just calling your franchisor when problems occur, why not give them a call when sales are going well and congratulate them on the excellent marketing support they have provided. You will be building goodwill and reinforcing their tendency to continue to put in good work for your benefit.

2. Having a Slack Attack

Nothing annoys a proud franchisor more than a business that looks run down and shabby due to a lack of effort by the franchisee.

On the other hand, by taking the maintenance of standards seriously you will almost guarantee the respect and support of your franchisor. In a franchise environment, slacking on operational standards is unlikely to win you many friends — or customers for that matter.

3. Singing Sinatra's Song

Frank Sinatra's "I Did It My Way" may be a song that franchisors love to sing. But it is not a tune they like to hear from their franchisees!

Experimenting with your franchisor's concept without prior consultation is bound to get you into hot water so be sure to use proper channels for trying out new ideas. If you are a particularly creative person, why not arrange to have your business used as a research and development site or join a product advisory team?

4. Behaving like a Clingon

As we learned in Chapter 13, all businesses must adapt to market forces and changing customer needs if they are to survive. When changes are proposed (as they inevitably will be from time to time) many franchisees will consider the changes with an open mind. However some will habitually reject the proposals outright without properly considering their merits.

This 'Clingon Reaction', clinging on to the past without any logical reason, even if it means becoming out of step with your customers, is not useful.

Rather than putting your franchisor in a position where they feel they have to drag you kicking and screaming, why not investigate the change with an open mind by asking questions and weighing up the risks and opportunities in a logical manner?

5. Falling prey to Bulletin Blindness

Franchisor staff regularly find themselves on the end of irate phone calls from franchisees who indignantly ask "Why wasn't I told?" The response is typically, "Francis, if you read the bulletin that was sent to you last week you will find all your questions have been fully answered".

Despite being busy and having to attend to 101 urgent details, it is vital that you take the time to read the information bulletins sent to you or posted onto your Intranet site. These will no doubt have been carefully prepared with important information on a range of topics to help you run a better business.

6. Blowing Up

If you have ever had a boil you will know how painful they can be. What happens is that the poison builds up under the skin, creating more and more pressure, until eventually it erupts with a vengeance.

Feelings of frustration and resentment can also build up and erupt in a tirade of poisonous abuse. This of course makes everyone feel awkward and can damage long term relationships. There are many practical tips throughout this book on how to manage the feelings of frustration that we all experience from time to time.

7. Playing Prisoner

When you bought into your franchise you hopefully made a properly researched and informed decision. The franchisor was not pushing you or twisting your arm. Yet some franchisees, when faced with difficult or challenging times, behave as though they are prisoners of the system or part of a conspiracy designed to take away their sense of responsibility or freedom.

As mature adults we are all responsible for our own decisions. Expecting others to make our decisions for us or playing the role of victim when things don't go as we expected serves no one's interests.

Franchisors are far more likely to respond in a constructive manner if, when faced with a business problem, you take the attitude, "I have some problems and I need some help and advice. But at the end of the day I accept that I have to take my own decisions."

In summary

There are specific franchisor behaviours and business practices that have been shown to improve or decrease the quality of the franchise relationship. Franchisees also need to take responsibility for the quality of the relationship. A franchisor interested in measuring and improving morale and satisfaction can gain a lot of useful information by conducting regular franchisee satisfaction surveys.

Action Tips:

- Conduct a franchisee satisfaction survey on what is working well and what could be improved at least every two years.

- If you are a CEO set up small group meetings with your franchisees, especially during times of significant change.

- Have the entire franchisor team confidentially fill out the Franchisor Relationship Checklist in this chapter, average the scores and look at any specific areas where a significant number of people ticked 'seldom' or 'never'.

- Have a sample of franchisees complete the same exercise and compare the findings.

- Franchisors — listen attentively to your franchisees, get things done, show them you care about their success, communicate directly, be competent in your job and maintain a positive approach.

- Franchisees — thank your franchisor occasionally for their good work, don't stray outside your franchisor's concept without permission, take the time to read the material your franchisor sends you, and take responsibility for what happens in your business.

CHAPTER EIGHTEEN
A Final Word from the Author

I hope this book has given you some inspiration and ideas that you can put to work in building a more profitable partnership with your fellow travellers in franchising.

If you are interested in receiving ongoing ideas on how to succeed in franchising I encourage you to visit www.franchiserelationships.com where you will find a range of publications, management tools and useful resources.

A profitable partnership is one that is of benefit to both parties — financially and personally. While most of the topics explored in this book are people focussed — to do with commitment, relationships, feelings and perceptions — I do not want you to get the impression that I underestimate the importance of good business disciplines and profitability.

Although a profitable franchise business does not always make for a happy franchisee, financial pressure will almost always expose weaknesses in a franchise relationship. Franchisees may put up with mediocre service, lack of support, little recognition and poor leadership from their franchisor if they are making healthy profits. However when the cash gets short, so does people's tolerance.

When discussing profitability issues it is well to remember that the franchisor must also be profitable if the franchise relationship is to be a stable one. There is often an assumption that because the franchisor is receiving regular royalties it must be profitable. The truth is that the costs in developing and maintaining a quality franchise system are substantial and it is not uncommon for larger franchisees to be more profitable than their franchisor.

In highlighting the human factors in successful franchising I also do not wish to down play the importance of good legal structures and agreements or the legitimate contribution that lawyers can make to good franchising practice.

However it has been the experience of nearly every franchisee and franchisor that I have spoken to over the years that, all things considered, it is the human issues that really make the difference. There has never been a financial, legal or marketing problem that could not be solved where people have been prepared to put their heads together in a spirit of cooperation and not give up until a satisfactory solution has been found.

I guess in a nutshell, my message is a simple one. Working together in an interdependent relationship often requires us to put aside our hobby horses, personal prejudices and vested interests and listen deeply to the legitimate needs and concerns of other people. This takes courage and a commitment to the relationship.

Yet if you can make this your working philosophy, and not give in to impatience or petty mindedness, I guarantee that you will have a stronger, more prosperous business that is better able to withstand the inevitable pressures of change and competition.

The simple truth is that your future success and prosperity will largely depend on how well you manage your relationships with other people.

About the
Franchise Relationships Institute

The Franchise Relationships Institute was founded for the purpose of helping franchisors and franchisees succeed together. All its work is based on the premise that a constructive relationship between franchisees and franchisor is essential for the success of both parties.

The Institute conducts an ongoing research program in collaboration with universities and franchise industry bodies into the factors that influence franchisee and franchisor success. From this research it has developed publications, talks, courses and tools including the following:

The Franchisor's Guide to Improving Field Visits — contains hundreds of ideas and strategies to help field managers ensure their visits to franchisees are adding value.

The Franchise E-Factor Book — provides franchisors with practical strategies for working with franchisees as they move through the six stages of the Franchise E-Factor (see Chapter 8).

How to Make Franchise Advisory Councils Work - this guide shows franchisors and franchisees how to establish or reinvent their FACs to be as effective as possible.

Conference presentations — Greg Nathan and his team are popular presenters. Each year they address franchisee and franchisor meetings all over the world on how franchisees and franchisors can build profitable partnerships and succeed together.

The ACE Franchisee Satisfaction Survey — a valuable performance improvement tool for the franchisor which measures the factors that drive franchisee Advocacy, Commitment and Engagement.

The Nathan Profiler — provides franchisors with a total system for measuring the suitability of prospective franchisees and preparing them for success.

The Franchisee Mentor — a diagnostic tool that identifies development and coaching needs for individuals and groups of franchisees.

The Multi-Unit Diagnostic — measures the readiness of existing franchisees to expand into additional units and provides coaching recommendations.

For more information about these products and the Franchise Relationships Institute go to:

www.franchiserelationships.com

To purchase bulk copies of Profitable Partnerships please contact us.

Email: info@franchiserelationships.com

Phone: +61 7 3510 9000

Postal Address: PO Box 8487 Armadale Victoria 3143 Australia